UNMASKED

Dare to be
the real you

Jon
Norman

— Endorsements —

"Jon and Chantel are dynamic leaders in this generation. The impact that SOUL Church is having across the community is remarkable. Their passion for social justice combined with their vision and sense of fun is wonderfully inspiring."
Revd Nicky Gumbel,
Holy Trinity Brompton

"Jon Norman is a great learner, follower, disciple, leader, and now it seems, he is an author too! Not only has he repurposed and empowered the local church to become a driving force within Great Britain, but he has also done it with his usual grace, audacity and aplomb. His humour, candour and insight in addressing the challenging issues within unmasked, not only make the book a must-read but easy to apply. This book can change your life!"
Pastor Glyn Barrett
Senior Pastor !Audacious Church
National Leader Assemblies of God Great Britain
Co-Chair Empowered21 Western Europe

"UNMASKED is a timely reminder that we can step out from behind the masks of fear, anxiety & insecurity into the life of freedom that God has called us to. Jon shares openly and vulnerably about how he removed some of the masks in his own life and moved forward with courage & conviction. I am grateful for Jon's leadership and friendship and pray that this book helps you remove the masks in your own life."
Benny Perez
Lead Pastor, ChurchLV

"At a time when the focus on masks dominates a global cultural narrative, creating division in part, and controversy in politics, my good friend Jon Norman addresses masks of much deeper significance: The masks that keep us alienated from ourselves and each other, which create ambiguity in our relationship with God. Jon's book will lead the reader to peel back the masks off their face and walk in the authentic Christian experience. Jon points out that this can only come from a fresh encounter with the living God. Jon is a passionate leader with a big vision, and an even bigger heart for the people he leads. This is a much needed book: Readable, timely and responsible. An honest book much needed for our times."

Ken Costa
Friend and Author

Jon Norman is a leader you can trust. We love that his thoughts have found their way onto the pages of this book, one that should be on the book shelf of anyone who cares about how we navigate the complexities of being who we are called to be, with authenticity, confidence and conviction.

Andrew & Louise Cherrie
Lead Pastors, Glow Church UK

In a world where we are bombarded by countless voices that influence our every step, it's often difficult to discern the voice of truth. Jon shows us how to cut through the noise and hear God's voice. This book is a must read.

Dr. Dave Martin
America's #1 Christian Success Coach & Best Selling Author

Jon Norman is the real deal. I never laugh as much as when I'm with him. This season has taught us all to remove the 'masks' we wear and this book will help us learn how to do that with confidence.

Martin Smith
Singer & Songwriter

Jon Norman can encourage and build up people like no one else I know. The genuine time, wisdom and love he has for others is extraordinary. I have no doubt that what he has written in this book will be life changing, and like everything else he does, it will point people to Jesus! I can't wait to get my copy!

David & Jacqui Cameron
Lead Pastors, Refuge Church, San Antonio Tx

"Jon is an incredible husband, father, leader and preacher but one of his stand out qualities is his continual commitment to lifting the lives of those around him. Jon has an incredible way of teaching truth in a simple, relevant and humorous way that will definitely add value, bring wisdom and lift your life to another level. It is with great joy and expectation that we get to recommend this book to you."

Phil & Lucinda Dooley
Hillsong Church, South Africa

"Jon Norman is an incredible pastor and leader who is passionate about seeing people become all that God has called them to be. His authenticity is inspiring. Nothing is off limits. Unmasked will build your faith, broaden your perspective, and help you walk in the freedom that God has for you."

Matt & Jill McCloghry
Lead Pastors at Colonial Church

"Jon Norman is one of the most consistent people I know: in discipline, in joy, in vision, in passion—he knows how to put one foot in front of the other. The man ran 7 marathons in 7 days, for crying out loud. Jon has mastered the secrets of the secret life. Any time he is talking about personal development, I'm all ears. This book, if patiently applied, will shortcut the distance between you and your destiny."
Nathan Finochio
Founder of TheosU & TheosSeminary

"Having known Jon for over a decade, we can wholeheartedly say he practices what he preaches. His life is his message and his love for people, his passion for the Church, his unwavering sense of Godly hope is inspiring and strengthens your soul.
We know this book will help people immensely because it is an extension of his life served over years gone and over years to come to help people find freedom!"
Dave & Abs Niblock
LIFE Church

"Unmasked is a timely guide to take off the masks that keep us bound and help you walk in freedom. With a powerful combination of inspiration and application, this book is for you."
Bolaji Idowu
Senior Pastor, Harvesters International Christian Centre, Lagos Nigeria

– Contents –

— Acknowledgements —

I would like to express my deepest gratitude to everyone who believed in me enough to make this dream a reality.

Chantel, you have and always will be, my best friend and have been a rock by my side for over 15 years. I love you.

Rob Whall I'm grateful for your investment in this project, your time, your input and your patience!

To my creative heroes Stuart Smith & Joyce Vacca who put graphics & beautiful imagery to these words.

Thank you to Katy Cooper and Steve Mawston, you are the best of the best for keeping me on track, giving honest feedback, editing, challenging with grace and encouraging me to the finish line.

Hannah Lipton, Nathan French, Brittany Sipling & Charlotte Cowell who have helped get the words of Unmasked out to the world, thank you.

Kobus Johnsen who without your knowledge, none of this would be possible. Thank you for guiding me through the processes of turning a book dream into a reality. You honour JESUS with your gift.

Finally to the readers of Unmasked, thank you for allowing me to speak into your journey, and having the courage to remove the masks and walk in freedom.

— Foreword —

To know Jon Norman is to love him. Both he and his wife Chantel are effervescent, infectious people who are hard not to love.

Warm-hearted, gracious, and humorous, they know how to have fun; but don't be fooled. Jon is passionate about the deeper things of God and he has an avid commitment to the Word of God, and it's clear that he and his beautiful wife, love the House of God. In 2014, Jon and Chantel accepted the Lead Pastor roles of an amazing life-giving church situated in Norwich, UK. They soon named the church SOUL Church and as Lead Pastors their visionary leadership, clarity of purpose, love of people, and commitment to Christ have led to them experiencing tremendous momentum and growth. I'm sure this is no coincidence as they have committed their lives to connecting people into relationship with Jesus Christ and helping people find their purpose in life.

I first met Jon and Chantel at Hillsong College where as single young people from different sides of the world, they fell in love and committed to serving God together, wherever He may lead. A few years later, as a "power couple", they served at Hillsong South Africa for several years under the leadership of Pastors Phil and Lucinda Dooley.

Jon has a disarming honesty, undergirded with the aforementioned healthy dose of humour, and his unique message and anointing speak across generations and cultures. Jon has confronted his own 'masks' to walk in the freedom and transparency he writes about, qualifying him to speak with authority and insight gained from his journey of faith and service to Christ and His Church.

Unmasked, is the story of personal identity, acceptance, and freedom in Christ. It is about unmasking the lies we believe about God, ourselves, and the world in which we live. Jon takes a deep dive into confronting the ten most common, yet destructive masks people wear (such as fear, rejection, shame, guilt and sin). Through personal examples including his own battle with anxiety, Jon unpacks the truth about our God-design and the true freedom we are assured.

Everyone has masks of one kind or another. A pastor's kid myself, with an impossible dream and the belief that God could do anything, as a child I struggled with insecurity and rejection that threatened to sabotage my dream and potential. I wasn't a good fit for school, spending more time daydreaming about the future beyond the classroom walls than I did learning. One of my teachers was so exasperated with me one day she announced, "Houston! You'll never amount to anything!" - driving home the lie, insecurity and rejection became part of my identity.

If I've learned anything, it is that no matter what life throws at you, whether people, circumstances or spiritual forces of darkness, God will not give up on you. He will never leave you in the mess. The unmasked life is not about perfection but acknowledgment of our weaknesses; recognising we are 'works in progress' in the process of transformation. On the Potter's wheel of life, our Heavenly Father's guiding hands of unconditional love are tirelessly moulding and shaping a vessel of honour.

God's ways are not our ways. Looking back over the many decades of my life, the twists and turns, unexpected encounters, setbacks and sacrifices, I am overwhelmed at His faithfulness to that young boy's dream despite the crippling masks; so grateful that God did not leave me in my weakness and ignorance - I could never have imagined what He had in store! A life of walking with God and believing Him at His Word, leaves me more convinced than ever that God is no respecter of persons – what

He does for one He will do for any who will commit to the journey with Him.

> *I can't tell you how much I long for you to enter this wide-open, spacious life. We didn't fence you in. The smallness you feel comes from within you. Your lives aren't small, but you're living them in a small way. I'm speaking as plainly as I can and with great affection. Open up your lives. Live openly and expansively!*
>
> *Don't become partners with those who reject God. How can you make a partnership out of right and wrong? That's not partnership; that's war. Is light best friends with dark? Does Christ go strolling with the Devil? Do trust and mistrust hold hands? Who would think of setting up pagan idols in God's holy Temple? But that is exactly what we are, each of us a temple in whom God lives.*
>
> 2 Corinthians 6:11-16 (MSG)

As Paul explained in his letter to the Corinthian church, the wide-open, spacious life is not automatic. It doesn't happen by chance or living small lives that never step beyond the safe and familiar. It is making one right choice after another in a life of partnership with our Creator, Saviour and Lord. And if ever there was a time to shake off our masks to live free and authentic lives, it is now.

As you explore these pages, I encourage you to trust God to weave the threads of your life into a truly glorious story of freedom and wholeness. Unmasked provides you with a practical pathway and 'prescription' for the life you were created to live. Each page systematically peels back the layers to uncover the masks you wear, confronts the beliefs that have kept them there, and guides you into the abundant life Jesus promised. It is my prayer that this book will help break the strongholds that keep you contained and liberate you into the wide-open and spacious life that awaits in Jesus all-powerful name.

Brian Houston
Global Senior Pastor
Hillsong Church

— Prologue —

2021, and everywhere we look we are surrounded by the sight of masks. Who would have thought just twelve months ago you would need to put on a mask just to purchase groceries, board a plane, or travel on a bus? Physical masks are in place to protect one another from coronavirus. In time, the mirage of masks will slowly disappear, but invisible masks which, unfortunately we can't see, will remain; it is these hidden masks that have the potential to reap havoc in our lives and cause us to stall, stop, and fall short of our destiny and who God has called us to be.

Recently, I was standing in line at Starbucks waiting to receive my tea, when for perhaps the first time it dawned on me the impact that masks can have in our lives. For those of us who have a smartphone, you will be familiar with the face recognition technology that allows you to unlock your phone, simply by looking into the camera. As I was standing in line, I went to unlock my phone, but to my frustration it wouldn't recognize my face because the mask I was wearing was covering the contours and shape of my face. The operating system had the capability to unlock the phone; however, because I was wearing a mask, my identity couldn't be revealed to the camera, and I wasn't fully recognised for who I really was. I could not be verified or validated, even though I owned the phone, because the mask I was wearing had inhibited my identity. The consequence was I couldn't get access to the apps and the resources that were rightfully mine and that I'd paid for because the mask stopped me from being recognised.

What happened in the Starbucks queue happens to you and me on a daily basis; we can't be recognised for who we really are because of the different masks we wear. God has given each of us a unique footprint, an ID, and a purpose. He has given us a standard operating system, made in the image of God, created in His likeness, and he has paid for us to own apps that will equip and resource us for our entire lives. Apps like love, joy, peace and security to name a few, but so often we can't access them because the mask inhibits us from living in the fullness of the identity Christ has paid for.

Whichever mask we wear and think looks good on us, they are never remotely close to who God created us to be. I wonder what mask comes to mind for you in this moment? For me, my humour can be a mask, and I hide behind my personality; someone asks me how I'm doing and I crack a funny joke to cover up the deeper things going on inside of me. A common response when we know there is a problem, but acknowledge there is an uncomfortable solution, is, *'This is just the way I am, and you just need to get used to it. Accept all of me or none of me'.* It might be the way you are, but it's not the way you have to stay, and often it's not the way God intended you to be. There is a side of me that everyone else sees depending on which mask I choose to wear in each given situation and circumstance. And then there is the real me. Like layers of an onion, as I peel them back, I discover the real me, the one God created me to be.

I truly believe that a war is happening over our identity right now. A war which has stopped us from living authentic, vulnerable and transparent lives, and is therefore robbing us from living life in all its fullness. In John's Gospel in the Bible, John records the words of Jesus warning us of the enemy's schemes to distort our identity and distract us from our purpose. He is known as *'the father of lies'* (John 8:44). The complete opposite of our Heavenly Father, revealed in Jesus, who said: *'I am the way, the truth and the life'* (John 14:6). Whereas the thief comes to steal, kill and to destroy, Jesus has come for us to have life, and life more abundantly (John 10:10).

Many people would wear masks during the time Jesus was alive and as He carried out His ministry. His greatest opponents were known as the Pharisees, a religious sect of Judaism, that would have the outward appearance of holiness but would be far removed from loving and meeting the needs of the people they were called to serve. Jesus in fact called them 'hypocrites' on many occasions. The word hypocrite comes from the Greek word hypokrites, "an actor" or "a stage player." It literally translates as "an interpreter from underneath", which reflects that ancient Greek actors wore masks and the actor spoke from underneath that mask. They were playing a role in public that was hiding who they were in private. Masks mattered to Jesus, and He was committed to taking them off.

The enemy always tries to take what God meant for good and pervert it, hurt it, or destroy it. That is why he is committed to tempting us to wear masks and camouflage who we are and to cause us to procrastinate from dealing with the underlying parts of ourselves we wish we could put in a drawer and hide away. It is for this reason I have decided to write this book *Unmasked*. It is God's desire for us to live in freedom. When we drop our masks, we experience and find our true identity. The greatest gift for you, and the greatest gift to the world around you, is you being the real you. We can never truly reflect God's glory until we take off our masks and live out authentic lives that express God's image through us, out into the world.

In this book, we will unpack ten of the most prevalent masks that I have personally struggled with — and I know many others have, too, that stop us from experiencing true freedom. It will be incredibly practical, and at times it will feel slightly uncomfortable, as we diagnose the symptoms that masks have on us, find the source, and then give a prescription of how to take off the masks we wear — once and for all. It is my belief, as you begin your journey of reading this book and take your next step, which is turning the page, you will start a process of transformation in your life. Through reading this book, you will learn that being yourself doesn't mean you are signing up or subscribing to a life of strength, surrendering our weakness to become the one who is made strong in the hands of God. As you recognise your masks and release the power they have over your life, it is my prayer that you will receive a fresh understanding of who you are in Christ; you are unconditionally loved by your Heavenly Father. Even though you're not perfect (join the club) and even though you might be an unfinished product, He loves you. Each one of these masks we will uncover are masks I have personally struggled with and, if I am honest, some of them I continue to battle with, but I believe we can remove them with God's strength. It's time to have an honest conversation, recognise some of the external masks we hide behind, and remove them!

At the end of each chapter, I have written a short prayer, which I encourage you to pray quietly or out loud, to help you and remind you that you can move forward with God's help.

Are you ready?

Chapter One
– *Fear Unmasked*

DO YOU ever feel fearful? I know I do. I don't mean to start this book in therapy mode, but I have to admit, I struggle with fear. When fear grips me, so much anxiety, panic and doubt streams through my mind. I can't flick fear off my shoulder and tell it where to go before focusing my attention back onto what is most important to me; instead, I have a relentless tug of war in my head and heart, a battle waging every moment of every minute of every day. I wonder whether you do, too?

Fear is designed to grip us, to paralyse us, to disable us, and to disarm us from walking out God's plan for our lives. Fear has become an epidemic of epic proportions in our world. Every day our news feeds saturate and bombard us with the uncertainty in our economy, in our leadership, and in our politics. It amplifies the unprecedented times we are in and the uncharted waters we all have to navigate. The headlines are clear:

'We have never been this way before!" "Prepare for the worst, hope for the best.'

Nearly every notification and news feed is designed to feed our fears and create a spiral of panic within us. Fear takes its hold on us whenever we believe that something undesirable, uncomfortable, and uncontrollable, is going to happen to us. At times, fear is irrational, and sometimes it is well founded. But no matter what the fear is, it always affects us in an unhealthy way.

Fear is nothing new; it has always played a part in the story of humanity and God. In the Bible, the most repeated commandment is the command to 'fear not'. Many people have counted how many times this command is mentioned in scripture, and there are three hundred and sixty-six! The command fills scripture, perhaps because God knows the widespread implications of fear in our lives. He knows that we have all kinds of fears. Fear taunts us, chanting our inadequacies, questioning our worth, and echoing our inferiorities back at us on a daily basis. Fear takes a foothold in our lives and then dominates our lives by becoming a stronghold. In turn, these strongholds paralyse us in our present, because we focus either on the fears that plant themselves in our past either or fears that might grab us in the future. Ultimately, the emotion you let lead you will determine the future you experience. Fear is never satisfied because it's like a compulsive addiction that will never volunteer to go away by itself. If you open the door even a little bit to your fear, it will take over every room in your life.

Fear is subtle; it doesn't always look like fear. Sometimes it is obvious like when our 'fight or flight' mechanism kicks in, and we know we are to run. But at other times, it doesn't grab us so overtly; it shows up as 'a thousand paper cuts'. One anxiety at a time, one worry that leads to stress, that leads to a sense of dread and leaves us feeling mentally, physically, emotionally, and even spiritually weak and exhausted. What do we do with these fears, and where do they come from? Disarming fear and developing our faith is not an immediate process but an incremental one. As we come up out of the pit of fear, we climb one step at a time, one experience at a time, one moment at a time.

So much material has been written around overcoming fear. Many resources are helpful and speak to fear's family members, (worry, anxiety and stress), but the end result tends to be the same. How do we dilute and soften the symptoms instead of over-coming them? It's as if they loosen the mask, as opposed to help-ing us take it off! The answer is seldom as simple as saying, "Fear, disappear". The great Christian author CS Lewis writes in his book 'The Lion, the Witch and the Wardrobe' (my kids' favourite movie ever): "All shall be done, but it may be harder than you think." Of course, we all wish that there was a vaccine that could make us immune from the pandemic of fear that pervades our lives, but in fact we need to dig deep and get to the root cause and unearth the root to our fears.

One of the primary reasons for our fear is how we have been conditioned. So often, fear originates from our upbringing and early experiences. Growing up, I think we all faced fear. I remember the fear of monsters in my back garden, the slightest noise during the night as I lay in bed had me imagining I was about to be invaded by an extraterrestrial force. Some nights, I was so full of fear I would run to my parents' bedroom, which was only 10 meters down the hallway, but as a child it felt like I was running the length of a marathon to get there safely! It reminds me about the story told of a man who had a morbid fear of thunder, so he went to see a psychiatrist. 'You have a condition called bronto-phobia," the doctor said. "It's silly to be afraid of thunder at your age. Just think of it as a drum roll in the symphony of life.' 'What if that doesn't work?' the man asked. The psychiatrist replied, 'Then do what I do. When you hear thunder, stuff cotton wool in your ears, crawl under the bed, and sing 'Mary Had a Little Lamb' at the top of your lungs until the thunder stops.' Many of our fears are based on our feelings, not on facts!

The second root of our fear is our habit of concealing what we are scared to uncover. Fear has destroyed more people's lives than any other mask, and that is why I am so committed to helping people take off the mask and live in freedom. Any time we conceal something that we are fearful of, we creep into deception, it hinders our ability to move forward in life, we feel a sense of shame and we feel as though we are 'not enough'. After all, we have a reputation to uphold, and we have relationships to manage. It is much easier to carry our burdens and baggage than to reveal them to the world. As we suppress our feelings and try to exude a sense of perfectionism, we keep our true self from getting out. We keep our masks on as we don't want the real 'us' to be revealed. We forget that God has wired us for a particular work; we have been custom built by design and crafted for our calling. These truths get crowded out by the noise of insecurity as we fear the real us will be exposed for all to see. We need to step out of these feelings and lay them down at the foot of the cross, before Jesus. This is so important for us to grasp, and take hold of, as when what is concealed is not confronted, callings can go unfulfilled.

Finally, our fear can be found in our desire to be controlling. Control is an illusion. We cannot control outcomes; we can only control our output. Yet, we grip tightly onto every situation and circumstance, suffocating the life out of relationships and our peace, because we want to make sure our experience lines up with our expectations. As we saw in our world in 2020, outcomes cannot be controlled. Control is the sense that I can hold up the world without God's help; it is unrealistic and irrational to fight for control, instead we are invited to surrender. If I am honest, as a leader I struggle with control and letting go; it is a rational fear as I justify it in my head that I am on the only one who can do it this way, so I refuse to let go. But actually, in doing this, I am adding more pressure to my life and not giving others the opportunity to move forward, so my fear has a huge negative impact on others. Fear is never satisfied with affecting you but will always impact others as well.

These three areas that I have just outlined as the origins for our fear all obscure our view of God. They dilute our confidence, and they crush our courage. But although fear can be a speed bump that slows us down, it should not be a stop sign that halts our progress and limits our potential. One of the ways in which we take off the mask of fear is to expose the fear that we are experiencing and bring it out of the shadows and into the light so that we can walk in freedom and experience true peace. With that in mind, let us look at some of the most prevalent fears many of us face in our lives.

Most of our fears fall into one of four categories:

THE FEAR OF FAILURE

In my opinion, there is not a more terrifying word in the human language or dictionary. In view of all transparency and vulnerability, I fear failure more than anything else. It is my greatest fear. I have to wrestle with this on a regular basis. I regularly ask myself the question: 'What if I fail as a dad'? You can read all the self-help books and parenting hacks on, 'how to be a great dad' and scan the 'prepare to be the best dad' books on the shop shelves, but until that little baby pops out, there is nothing which can prepare you for it. No parent wants to get it wrong, but let's be honest, every mum and dad along the parenthood journey gets it wrong. We are not perfect. We put the nappy on the wrong way or we say something we regret. Tiredness kicks in, patience moves out, and before long, the newly established rhythms that we are finally used to, must give way to another stage in our child's development. Either sleeping patterns change, or their needs and desires are no longer met. You are constantly adjusting and adapting, and it is a scary time.

The award for biggest parenting blooper must go to my parents! My mum and dad told my sister and I the story about when we were babies. Both my parents had got home late one night, and my mum thought my dad was getting us both out of the back of the car. Dad, however, thought he was just getting one of us out. They went up to bed, and my sister spent a portion of the night on the back seat in the drive! I'm sure one of those parenting books would have suggested bringing the kids in before you go to bed, hey! Before I became a father, I was the best dad. I could tell you how to stop a baby crying, I could describe how to keep your kids quiet in a movie; I could run off all the ways you can entertain them all day without them throwing a tantrum, and then guess what... I became a dad! And like all fathers from time to time, I thought I have failed.

Parenting is a lot tougher in real time than the tricks of the trade sold to us from the Waterstone's bookshelves! My daughter only recently said "Dad, why can't we have more fun? Why are you always at work? Why are you always on the phone?" That really hurt me, and it was a reality check for me! In that moment, I felt like a failure. It started a spiral of despair, as I asked myself: 'Am I living by priorities or pressures? 'Is this lifestyle sustainable?' 'What will my children remember about their own childhood, and me as their dad?' 'Have I failed at parenting?' Perhaps you sometimes feel the same in an area of your life that matters to you. Failure creates a perpetual cycle of paralysis in our lives — fear of failed exams, fear of a failing marriage, fear of redundancy. The fear of failure is listed as being in the top ten worst human fears; it ranks alongside the fear of public speaking, of disapproval, and of death.

Our fear of failure is taught. We were not born with a fear of failure. We learned to be afraid of failing somewhere down the line, and that clothed itself in shame and an inclination to 'win at all costs' to avoid being exposed or truly seen. We spend our whole lives fearing failure, and the fear of failure can become our ultimate failure. You would be shocked at the dialogue and discussions I have with myself on a daily basis. Human beings have around sixty thousand thoughts every single day, and scientists tell us that eighty percent of those thoughts are negative. We are wired to want to win and to want to avoid failure at all costs. I don't just have a fear of failure when it comes to my parenting; I also have my own fear of failure when it comes to pastoring a church. I often think to myself and say to my wife Chantel, 'What if I fail with SOUL Church?' As I write this book, we are in the process of raising funds to build an £8 million new 1200 capacity facility for our church, which

sounds very nice, and I am so excited about the prospect of help-
ing more people and seeing more folks find the love of Jesus, but
the soundtrack called fear plays over and over in my head and
says to me: 'What if I can't raise the finance? What if we have built
it too big? What if we build too small? What if we build it and no
one comes?' Then there is the week-to-week fear of failure. Just
like most pastors I speak to, one of my biggest fears is 'will people
show up today? What if they all suddenly disappear and move to
another church? What if they didn't appreciate my message last
week? What if, what if, what if...' And the track just keeps playing
in my head.

THE FEAR OF REJECTION

The second common fear is a fear of rejection. We will cover the
fear of rejection in detail in the next chapter, but fear of being
rejected is so real in our lives. In our social media crazed world,
we live in fear of people not accepting our posts, re-tweeting our
thoughts, or ignoring what we have to say and what we stand for.
We are longing for love but living for likes. The fear of rejection
doesn't limit itself to social media either: there's the fear of being
left on the shelf and being single for the rest of our lives, the fear
of being left out of the team, of not being good enough, or of being constantly compared to others. Fear of rejection has stopped
me many times from writing this book. What if no one buys it?
What if they read the first chapter and put it down? (don't you
dare :-) We must remember that rejection is often re-direction.
Some of the heroes in the Bible, Joseph, David and Moses — were
all rejected. I'll pause on rejection for now as I want to unmask it
more in our next chapter.

THE FEAR OF LOSS

More so than ever, we are living at a time when people have experienced great loss and encountered much pain. Thousands of people have lost loved ones during the global pandemic and the fear of loss is so real in our lives. Loss isn't something we can necessarily plan for and we never really know when it is going to arrive. We can't control death, and we can't control the grief that comes with it. Often, it is what we can't control that we fear the most. Once we have experienced the pain of loss and over a period of time managed to finally come to terms with it and move forward, the very thought of having to face that again understandably fills us with fear.

THE FEAR OF THE UNKNOWN

None of us know what tomorrow may bring. It sounds a bit cliché, like something you would read on the back of a Starbucks cup, but in my experience the saying rings true. You can plan your day with the best intentions in the world. Wake up early, get the kids ready for the day, have your road trip all mapped out, and you are ready to execute your meticulously planned itinerary, and then calamity strikes. Your child gets sick, the weather turns for the worst, your car breaks down and your favourite mother-in-law (I've got a special spot for my mother-in-law at Christmas: down the garden behind the shed. Don't get mad at me; I'm joking – Queenie knows I love her, really!) gives her unneeded opinion of your parenting skills. Suddenly, we go into free fall.

As I'm writing this chapter, our world is facing unprecedented measures with COVID-19. It is an invisible enemy which none of us knows the magnitude of, yet it's not just a physical pandemic we face but also a fear pandemic. Fear of the unknown is rampant in every home, business, hospital and community. Our fear is justifiably and firmly rooted in the fact that we don't know what's next, and we don't know when this will come to an end. Everyone just wants to wake up tomorrow as if it was all a bad dream, but every morning we wake up and it isn't.

Our minds never seem to go to the best case but the worst-case scenario; our imaginations take us to places which can cause us torment and irrational thoughts spring up like weeds in an unkept garden. It is the unknown which caused people in the thousands to rush to the supermarkets and buy up every last toilet roll. It is fear of the unknown which causes global stocks to plunge overnight. Fear of the unknown is worse than the reality of the known; we can handle, control, plan, rebuild, heal the known but the unknown is out of our control. Whatever we can't control, we fear (that will tweet).

Now that we have diagnosed four of the most common fear masks that we wear, let's look at how we can take the mask of fear off. What might this look like, and how can it be achieved?

I was never a huge fan of biology at school. I enjoyed the Bunsen burner (nice little earner), and I occasionally had a laugh (bubble bath) during the 'reproductive system' classes, but most biology lessons can be remembered for each student picking up a microscope from the shelf, placing the instrument on the work station, and then spending half the lesson, turning the dial, trying to zoom in on some obscure cell placed on a petri dish, that our teacher assured us had 'ground breaking' implications for our lives and the future of humanity. The reality was, we were focusing our microscope on a seemingly small detail and it simply produced a much larger version of a very small image.

I have noticed that many people have the propensity to do likewise when faced with something that makes them fearful. I call it having a 'microscope mentality'. They focus their lens on the problem or situation before then turning the dial on the side, magnifying the problem, making it bigger and bigger, until nothing else can be viewed except the uphill challenge that's before them. A microscope by its very nature is to produce a larger version of a small object. It disregards everything that surrounds the image being looked at, and focuses in, as if it was the only thing in the world worth looking at.

When you have a 'microscope mentality' you tend to focus in on your fear, the 'what if' scenarios skipping around your head become louder and louder, and it's almost impossible to tune in to another frequency. We let our circumstances define our theology instead of letting our theology define our circumstances. What we magnify, we get more of. If I magnify fear in my life, I become more fearful, If I magnify faith, I produce more faith. In my own pastoral experience, and my own personal life, I know the temptations of adopting a 'microscope mentality'. It can feel easier to narrow our focus on the problem at hand instead of seeing our circumstances and situations in light of a bigger picture and a much bigger God. For us to overcome our fears, we must put down the microscope and pick up the telescope.

A telescope is used to magnify something big and significant; it takes into consideration the big picture and views things on a much larger scale. When we pick up a telescope, we focus on how big God is and how small our problems are in comparison. Our fears and problems are put in proportion and their correct perspective. As we talk to God and get to know Him more, we will adopt the telescope mentality. When this happens, we can acknowledge that we have fears, but we will not allow the fear to have us! We have to intentionally fix our focus on what magnifies God and what minimises our fears. We are all faced with a choice in what we focus on and which instrument we choose to pick up when we are faced with fear. The subject of our focus will ultimately shape our lives. Faith is the opposite of fear. Living by faith doesn't mean that we ignore our circumstances, but it means that we choose to focus on God and believe that He is greater than anything we are going through. Many times, we are overpowered and overcome by fear because we keep feeding our fearful thoughts, and as we feed them they are eating us alive!

The apostle Paul was masterful at choosing to focus on God. He was not without his troubles. However, after being imprisoned, investigated and subjected to impending death, Paul found a prescription for fighting fear with faith.

Firstly, he instructs us to rejoice. Philippians 4:4 tells us to, '*Rejoice in the Lord always*.' Rejoice simply means to 'take delight in'. He's so serious about it that he repeats the command: '*I will say it again: Rejoice!*' As Paul sits in a Roman prison, he believes that it's possible to praise God wherever we find ourselves and whatever we are fearful of.

Secondly, Paul calls us to release our fears and anxiety. He says in Philippians 4:6, 'Do not be anxious about *anything, but in every situation, by prayer and petition, with thanksgiving, present your requests to God*.' Prayer facilitates us experiencing true peace by functioning as a sort of pressure release valve, draining the anxieties that build up within us into the care of God. Freedom and peace await those who are willing to give their worries to God and leave them in His hands.

Finally, when we release our anxiety, we can redirect our thoughts towards God. Paul turns his attention to what we should be thinking about. In verses 8-9, Paul tells us specifically what we should be meditating on because what we focus on becomes magnified in our minds:

'Finally, brothers and sisters, whatever is true, whatever is noble, whatever is right, whatever is pure, whatever is lovely, whatever is admirable - if anything is excellent or praiseworthy - think about such things.'

What happens when we release our anxiety and redirect our thoughts? Paul says, *'...the God of peace will be with us.'* (Philippians 4:9). We do not need to let our situation and circumstances rob us of our peace. God has placed His peace and presence within us so that whatever we face, be it prison or otherwise, we can hold onto our peace in the presence of fear.

Arthur Gordon is an author in his late seventies. He came to one of these bleak periods in his life that many people experience from time to time, a sudden drastic dip where he felt stale and he had flat lined emotionally and spiritually. His energy had disappeared, his enthusiasm had dissipated. Finally, after struggling for months and months, he went to see his doctor to see if there was a physical cause. The doctor realised it was nothing physical, but it was to do with the fact Arthur had pushed himself for too long. So, the doctor asked Arthur what his favourite childhood memory was, Arthur responded: 'Going to the beach!' 'Go to the beach, then!' his doctor replied. 'Go for a whole day, just by yourself. I am writing you four prescriptions. I want you to open these at nine, twelve, three, and six.' Arthur wasn't given any pills or medicine, just a simple set of instructions. Once the doctor wrote them out, and gave them to Arthur, he set off to the beach.

Arthur went to the beach and tore open the first prescription at 9am, and it said: 'Listen carefully.' For three hours, Arthur just listened. He listened to the sound of God's creation, he embraced the silence, and ignored any sense of distraction. After a while, he felt peace, and the still small voice of the Holy Spirit began to speak to him. At noon, Arthur opened the second prescription, and it said: 'Try reaching back.' He thought back to those moments in his life where the blessings of God were most tangible to him. Moments of awe, celebration and wonder, and he began to re-live the happiest moments in his mind. At 3pm, he opened the third prescription which said: 'Examine your motives.' He had a moment, an epiphany of sorts, where he realised in a flash of certainty, 'if ones motives are wrong, nothing can be right. If you do the right thing for the wrong reasons in the Kingdom of God, it doesn't count.' Then finally at 6pm he opened the fourth and final prescription; it said: 'Write your worries in the sand.' Arthur found a stick and started to write out the problems, fears, worries, issues and frustrations, and then the tide came in. Sure enough, literally as if the doctor had perfectly planned it, the tide washed them all away.

Most of us struggle with fear. Taking off the mask of fear doesn't mean you'll never feel afraid again, but it does mean that you can have confidence in facing your fears and trust that you can overcome them with the help of Jesus. You can feel secure in God's grip on you, you can rest in His protection over you, and you can live with courage that He will come through for you. Whether our fears come from our conditioning, concealing, or controlling, let's pray together today that the tide of God's Spirit would wash over our hearts and minds, our fears will be rinsed away, our faith will be amplified, and we will rediscover, re-energise and re-engage with our God-given identifies.

Father God, I recognise today I have been wearing the mask of fear for too long. With your help, I choose to take off the mask of fear and to take hold of your courage and strength. You who are in me, is greater than He that is in the world. I receive your freedom and liberty today, and I take off the mask of fear once and for all! Amen.

Chapter Two
– *Rejection Unmasked*

IN 2018, I had the privilege of being invited to speak at Hillsong Conference at the prestigious O2 arena. There were thousands of people in attendance, and the main stage speakers included my Pastor, Brian Houston, Chris Hodges, John Gray and others. The way the schedule had been put together meant I was to speak after Pastor Brian, and John Gray was the night before. I remember as if it was yesterday, the feelings I felt thirty minutes before I was scheduled to speak. I was utterly overwhelmed and felt unbelievably intimidated; it was as if I had received a blow to the stomach. My chest was tight, and as I leant over my seat with my head rested in my palms, a whirlwind of emotions began to surface in my heart and mind as I waited to be called up. I pictured the arena in my mind's eye, and I was confronted with the questions: 'Why me God? What do I have to share and impart to them?' I now realise what I felt was a huge sense of what psychologists have called 'imposter syndrome'. People who struggle with imposter syndrome believe that they are undeserving of their achievements or the opportunities that come their way. They feel that they aren't as competent or intelligent as others might think, that they will be found out for 'who they really are' and that soon enough, people will discover the truth about them.

I felt a strong sense as I sat in the arena, preparing to take my place on stage, that I shouldn't be doing what I was doing. I was anticipating rejection. What triggers this emotion is often past experiences, previous words spoken to us, that have left an indentation in our hearts and mind. Whatever it was that triggered this emotional reaction in me, brought me to the end of myself, and it was the darkest half hour I have ever experienced in my entire life. In that moment, I said to God: 'I cannot do this without you. I need you to show up. This was not my idea! I need a supernatural touch from you'. By God's grace, I received the touch, and I was encouraged that many people were blessed and impacted by the talk I shared. What stands out for me through this experience is the rejection and inadequacy I felt. It caused me to want to withdraw and isolate myself and to essentially hide. This is what we see in the opening scenes in the Bible in the Garden of Eden, Adam and Eve hiding themselves from God, and we've been building fig leaves ever since to protect and cover ourselves from others.

For me it was the O2 arena, but such a feeling of imposter syndrome shows up in every area, every day of our lives. We can anticipate rejection before we decide whether to share our point of view in a meeting. We can anticipate rejection as we share our vulnerabilities, struggles and weaknesses with other people. We can anticipate rejection as we put ourselves out there and try to pursue a dream or a goal, or initiate a conversation with someone we fancy or want to ask on a date; I've been there before and it hurts, Chantel knocked me back three times before she eventually saw the light. Rejection creeps up on us, jumps on our backs, and causes us to fall to the floor as we shut down mentally, physically and emotionally. It can be difficult to get back up when the weight of past experiences and words from others press so forcefully against us. When we stay down on the ground, it can feel almost impossible to remove the mask of rejection from our faces, and we convince ourselves the only option is to concede to the emotions and feelings we feel and tap out!

You will have all heard the nursery rhyme 'sticks and stones will break my bones, but words can never hurt me.' Let's be honest, who wrote that? I'd love to put my arm round the writer's shoulder, invite him to sit down for a green tea with me, and as he takes his first sip, look him in the eyes and say to him: 'What on earth were you thinking when you wrote that line you numpty?' Because it's wrong; words do hurt—in fact, words sting. One of the greatest privileges of the journey for Chantel and I serving in our roles as Senior pastors at SOUL Church has been listening to hundreds of people over the years share their story and oftentimes, their struggles. Having been involved in building the local Church for over two decades and drawing alongside people pastorally and listening to their challenges and obstacles, I have personally observed that so many people's lives can't progress, move forward, or change for the better, because they are wearing the life-anchoring mask that is rejection. Rejection has a way of stopping people's lives moving forward like no other.

When we hear this word, our minds can automatically go back to a time, a place or a person when we felt rejected. Rejection jumps out in so many different ways. When I teach on rejection, I will often ask for a show of hands to see how many have been hurt through rejection, and without exception it's always one hundred per cent of the room.

In 2019, I completed running seven marathons in seven days. Yes, that isn't a typo, SEVEN twenty-six-mile races. Some call me bonkers, others think I'm a glutton for punishment. The truth is I am completely bonkers, but I also had a strong conviction to do it to raise much needed funding for our new SOUL Church community facility. I spent hundreds of hours in preparation training during the twelve months building up to the main event. There were many incidents during the process that stick out in my mind, but one Saturday morning's training session jumps out in particular. Like all keen runners, lycra and Vaseline (I will spare you the details) are your best friends (perhaps not the Vaseline). They were there to be a help to me not a hindrance. Or so I thought! As I came running around the corner, there was a group of high-school students, and they look at me, point at me and start making inappropriate comments about my posterior and attire. Talk about rejection! That hurt; in that moment, as a forty-year-old husband and father, it was like being back in high school—words can really hurt, even from snotty-nosed teenagers!

According to experts, we are bombarded with thirty-five thousand messages a day. Everywhere we turn and everywhere we look, someone is trying to get our attention. Every politician, advertiser, journalist, family member, and acquaintance has something to say to us. Every day, we are faced with emails, text messages, billboards, television, movies, radio, Twitter, TikTok, Facebook and blogs. Add to these newspapers, magazines and books. Our world is cluttered with words. How do we choose which messages to tune in to and which ones to tune out? I have read that, on average, most people speak about sixteen thousand words a day. If you transcribed those words, they'd fill a three-hundred-page book, longer than the very book you hold in your hands or swipe on your digital device! At the end of a year, you would have an entire bookcase full of words. In a lifetime, you would fill a library. But how many words of people have caused others and us to feel a sense of rejection? Words hurt, words sting, and words can cause rejection in our lives, and those speaking them don't always know what it's doing to us, but it triggers within us deep layers of hurt that end up planting deep roots of rejection in our hearts and minds.

I remember when I was fourteen years old. It was Valentine's Day and I walked into my school classroom to see a pink envelope on my desk with my name on it. My heart leapt, my palms began to sweat, and as I picked up the letter, my hand began to shake. THIS WAS IT! THIS WAS THE MOMENT I had waited my whole fourteen-year-old life for! Suddenly I felt three inches taller, my chest was puffed out, and I was aware that everyone in the room was looking at me. 'Oh yes, you look over.... Yes, you all enjoy this... That's right, it's a card.... A card, for ME. This is my moment. This is what dreams are made of!' As I picked up the envelope opened it up, I was starting to imagine who the card was from. That little honey in my biology class or a secret admirer that's been watching Jonny Norman over the past term.

As I opened the card, I started to read:

"Roses are red...violets are blue..."

I was thinking this is incredible, my mind raced in real time: "COME ON, get to the point!!!!" And boom... I read the final words that hit me and left a lasting mark of pain, even to this day: "Umbrellas get lost and so should you".

How could such potential and promise unravel within seconds before my very eyes? My heart sank, and my first valentine resulted in a deep sense of rejection. Where once I felt loved, I now felt rejected. Where once I felt secure, I felt rocked. Where once I felt sure of my happy future, I now felt lonely and unsure of myself. I was fourteen, and even then I understood and experienced rejection in a world where we are all longing to be loved. Rejection can steal the best of who I am by reinforcing the worst of what's been said to me.

Social media has been the best and worst commodity of the last decade. I am told Facebook is now the world's largest country and is even considering creating its own currency due to so many followers and advertisers, with Instagram being just behind them in second place, as the second largest nation.

Of course, social media connects the world, and makes a big, wide world a small and accessible one. A few years back, I was able to reconnect with some long-lost cousins and find some of my alumni friends from school and college. The positives definitely outweigh the negatives. However, it's important to remember that social media is supposed to be our servant, and never our master. As dopamine (the pleasure hormone) is released every time we swipe, scroll, and stream, we are conditioning and training our minds and hearts to put more weight on what we see on social media than the truth about who we are. We constantly feel the need for approval, likes, comments and new followers. In a world longing for love, we end up settling for likes.

We have all had those moments when we did an Instagram Live and only five people logged on, or we uploaded a really cool picture and accomplishment, and the likes were slow to follow. We begin to feel a sense of rejection, and it robs us of what we have been called to do. We say to ourselves, "I can't believe they didn't like that photo I put up. Why do they have more followers than me?" Social media has created a world where we crave more and then ask questions internally when our experiences don't match our expectations.

Honesty moment: after I have spoken to large crowds and the first thing I've done is rushed off the stage to seek approval from my social media, but the irony is however much approval is waiting it's never enough—our human desire always craves for more.

Recently I reached out to an old friend on social media to try to re-connect, only to find out I had been blocked. In that moment, the pain was real you start questioning and relieving what you think you could have done, would have done and should have done. Rejection isn't just an emotion we feel, it's a message that's sent to the core of who we are, causing us to believe lies about ourselves, others and even God.

Rejection is mask no one was created to wear for long. It crushes the very person God created us to be. One of the wisest men who ever lived was a sage called King Solomon, and in his book of wisdom he writes: Proverbs 18:14 'A *man's spirit sustains him in his sickness, but a crushed spirit* who can bear?'

Rejection is a crusher which no one is immune to. King Solomon explains that we can bear physical sickness, but a crushed spirit caused by rejection is impossible to live with. So how do we recover from rejection? It would serve us well to remember that rejection was a part of Jesus' daily reality. People laughed at Him. People rejected Him. Jesus wasn't immune to rejection; throughout his whole life—from the very beginning to the crucifixion—

He suffered unprecedented rejection. Before He even arrived on Earth as a baby in the manger, He was rejected; the Christmas story begins with rejection, and the Easter story is centred on Jesus being rejected.

Joseph, the father of Jesus, was born in Bethlehem, grew up there, studied there, worked there, and all his life-long friends and family resided there. It would have been an easy decision to go back to have their first child amongst loved ones. To make matters even easier there had been a census requiring citizens to go back and register in their home town. So Joseph and his heavenly pregnant wife arrived back in their home town, excited to spend the next month or so with their nearest and dearest to share the most exciting moment of their lives, child birth.

In the second chapter of Luke's Gospel, we are told that Mary brought forth her firstborn Son, wrapped Him in swaddling clothes, and laid Him in a manger because there was no room for them in the inn. But why? You shouldn't be looking for a hotel if you have family close by. Mary had the baby out of wedlock, and Joseph's family was ashamed, so everyone had rejected them. In Jewish law, Mary could have actually been stoned to death for becoming pregnant out of wedlock. There was no room at the inn, no loved ones surrounding or supporting them, but far deeper than that was the fact that there was no acceptance from their loved ones. Maybe some of you can relate to being rejected by family or loved ones and it has caused you to wear a mask as a means of self-protection.

Isaiah 53:3 tells us that Jesus was despised and rejected by humanity. A man familiar with our pain and suffering. This shows us that throughout Jesus' life and ministry he experienced rejection. The religious leaders rejected His teaching. The Jewish people rejected Him as their Messiah. Even Peter rejected the way in which Jesus would establish His Kingdom and go to the cross! At critical junctures in Jesus' life, people misunderstood Jesus. Rejection was Jesus' everyday reality. Because this was Jesus› reality, He is the perfect person for us to turn to when rejection is, or has been, a reality for us. Jesus understands and teaches us from that tender place of knowing the pain of rejection personally.

But with every rejection that Jesus faced, we see Him respond with movement towards His ultimate goal. Jesus chose to remain steadfast amidst the rejection He experienced. When asked permission to get even, Jesus decided to use it as a teachable moment for His disciples. As we fast forward a few chapters to the ultimate rejection, when Jesus is taunted by those that He came to save on the cross, He asks God the Father to forgive them for their lack of understanding.

Jesus' actions reiterate His decision and desire to delight in doing His Father's will. Jesus knew that His purpose had been uniquely given to Him by the Father; as long as He knew He was accepted by God, He could be strong enough to ignore the rejection of other people. The focus and motivation of all the actions of Jesus fulfilled His desire to do the will of His Heavenly Father. Therefore, in each situation that He was rejected, His focus and His resolve never changed. He was able to do this because His unity with the Father surpassed all else. Scattered throughout the four gospels, Jesus intentionally connects with His Father and communicates with Him on a regular basis through prayer.

Christ's last human act before His death was one of acceptance. The thief next to Him on the cross deserved to die; he had committed real crimes against his community. Yet, Jesus looked at him and said: 'Today you will be with me in paradise.' This was the ultimate act of acceptance, even when Jesus was feeling rejected. It was just hours earlier that Pilate had presented Jesus (John 19:5) to a hostile crowd for their input into what should happen to Jesus. The same crowd whom He loved, fed, healed and befriended, were now shouting: "Crucify him! Crucify him." (Luke 23:21). Jesus went to the cross not only carrying our sin, our shame, our grief and our sorrows, but the heaviest weight of them all, the weight of rejection.

So how do we begin to take off the mask of rejection in our own lives? Firstly, through prioritising prayer. I like to look at prayer in a similar way to my relationship with Chantel, my wife. If you were to observe my relationship with Chantel, and you saw us speak to each other in the morning, but then we didn't connect throughout the day, you would think we were missing out on a key part of being married to each other. We wouldn't be supporting each other throughout the day; we wouldn't be communicating about the needs, wants and desires for our children. We certainly wouldn't be encouraging each other and speaking life into our marriage. That's why we have concentrated, focused time together, but we also have a continuous flow of conversation throughout the day.

We text each other, we send one another a cheeky emoji, we throw voice memos back and forth and FaceTime when we can. I like to see it as throwing another log in the fire so that our relationship can continue to burn bright, but also warm others as we live and lead by personal example. Of course, we don't get it right every day (I do must days but Chantel sometimes struggles :-), but we are intentional. Similarly, if we were to only text back and forth, without carving out and setting aside concentrated time together, like a date night, we would feel as though we haven't fully caught up with each other or be aware of how the other person is doing. Therefore, in our most important relationships, we need both concentrated and focused time together, but also continuous flow.

The same is true in our relationship with God. He simply wants us to go to Him and spend time with Him, to share how we feel, and to hear His voice, as well as to speak with Him throughout the day. If we do this, it will remind us of who we are, it will release us from the fear of rejection, and it will rekindle our love for Him and strengthen our resolve to walk out a resilient faith. Jesus knew this, so in those times when He was rejected by others, He could approach God and receive direction, comfort and ultimately affirmation for all He had endured and all He was about to endure. One of the key principles I try to live out in my everyday life, is living by priorities and not by pressures. A key priority is seeking out time to prioritise my relationship with God, which allows me to recalibrate after I have been rejected. This isn't an occasional act, but a regular discipline.

At this stage in the chapter, you might be thinking: 'Thanks Jon, you have given language to what I experience on a regular basis, and my fear of rejection is ever before me and ever trying to weigh me down. But how do I remove this fear of rejection?' Well, I believe practically speaking, we can get back up. We can predetermine, preload and preempt our responses to rejection according to what God says to us and what God has said about us. I have a simple strategy that disarms rejection from having a hold on me and helps me to direct my focus onto the affirmation I have already received from my Father in Heaven. It's simply, 'delete and download'.

The only possible opportunity rejection has to download intimidation and lies into my heart and mind is if I copy and paste it over the reality of God's truth spoken over my life. If I allow rejection to delete the memory of the fact I have been chosen by God and have been given a purpose to fulfil, then I download all the negative feelings that are associated with rejection. I download the weight of words and opinions from people that take up storage space, taking room that's designed for me—space for the truth God has already spoken over me. It is no coincidence that when Jesus was in the wilderness being tempted he shook off all the enemies temptations, in both form and function, by the scriptural truth: 'It is written....' (Matthew 4). Each time the enemy appeared to delete the truth of what Jesus knew in His heart, Jesus countered it by holding onto the truth He had already downloaded and what had been declared when He rose up out of the Jordan river, 'This is my beloved Son, with whom I am well pleased' (Matthew 3:17).

I truly believe, at the root of all rejection, we are ultimately being lured into questioning in our hearts whether we are enough and whether who we are, and what we have to offer, will make us accepted. Of course, the tools that the devil uses to shape rejection in our lives look different for each of us, but the details matter less than the destructive effect of experiencing rejection in our lives. We must choose to preload our minds and hearts with God's Word, remembering that we must never allow ourselves to get dragged down to the level of people's perception and opinion of us. If you know who you are, what others say about you is less significant, and the implications aren't so soul destroying. If I look in the mirror in the morning and say to myself:

I am called.
I am God's child.
I am truly loved by the Father.
I am validated not by what I do but whose I am.
I am forgiven.

I can truly receive and believe that acceptance is what I have and what God has in mind for me. I have discovered in my own life that recovering from past rejection is not a one-time event; rather it is a continuous, ongoing journey that demands I focus on the freedom I now have as a Christian. Every day I have to choose not to let rejection hang a big question mark over what I know to be true about who I am. I need to press my roots down deeper and deeper in the soil of truth that enables me to ignore rejection and embrace who I am.

Many people hold onto the mask of rejection because they feel unwilling or unable to forgive those that have overlooked and undervalued them. When they finally understand and apply forgiveness to the person that has rejected them, they experience freedom. As Paul writes to one of the churches in the New Testament, *"who the son sets free is free indeed."* (John 8:36). This is a process we can't ignore if we want to become the people God has created us to be. I would like to end this chapter by outlining the process we can take to forgive those that have hurt us so that we can finally unmask rejection in our lives.

Firstly, we must recognise that we have been forgiven by God our Father and that we rejected Him. Once we understand the depth of the distance our weaknesses and wrongdoing placed between us and God, and once we get a glimpse of the pain and sacrifice He made to restore fellowship with us after we rejected Him, we should not hesitate to forgive others. If we comprehend God the Father's forgiveness toward us but refuse to forgive those who've wronged and rejected us, then we are like the ungrateful servant described by Jesus in Matthew's Gospel. This ungrateful servant's huge debt had been wiped out and forgiven, and yet the servant immediately went onto demand repayment for a debt that someone owed him. The fact that God the Father has forgiven me even though I rejected Him first encourages, inspires and instructs me to follow His example when I have been rejected by others. This not only frees them from my judgment and bitterness, but it helps release me of my pain and the shame associated with rejection.

Second, it is important to release the person that has rejected you from the debt that we feel is owed to us. Many of you might be familiar with Chantel's story of forgiveness. As a young girl, she was sexually abused by someone close to her which left so much pain, anger and resentment as she grew older. This began the long journey of healing, re-establishing trust, and it wasn't an easy journey for Chantel. Like Chantel, we must enter into the pain and brokenness of our situation. We must begin to allow God to re-build our lives from the ruins and trust God, in the midst of the pain, that Christ ultimately has a purpose.

Thirdly, we must accept people as they are and release them from any responsibility to meet our wants and needs. We all know someone who blames feelings of acceptance or rejection on others; you may even be like that yourself. Certain individuals can make or break your day depending on the amount of attention they pay you. This is a common trait in those who are unable or unwilling to forgive. However, when we decide to forgive as an act of the will, we absolve others of any responsibility to meet our needs.

Fourthly, we can view those we've forgiven as opportunities and lessons in our lives. God uses situations and people to help us grow in our understanding of His grace. The Old Testament Bible character, Joseph, certainly grasped this principle. Joseph was thrown in a pit and sold into slavery by his brothers because they rejected him, and they were jealous of him. However, this rejection redirected him to the task God had for his life: to be the prime minister of Egypt. When Joseph was finally reacquainted with his brothers, he saw his brothers and their rejection of him as instruments God used to place him in a position to save his family during famine. His brothers feared what he might do to get even, but he responded, '*You meant evil against me, but God meant it for good in order to bring about this present result, to preserve many people alive*' (Genesis 50:20).

Fifth, when possible, we are to re-establish contact with estranged friends, former co-workers or family members, and an apology is a good place to start. We should do our part to re-store connection with those who've hurt us. Once forgiveness is complete, releasing our pain and being around that person will be much easier. Over time, and with the help of her Heavenly Father and some incredible people, Chantel's been able to overcome, and now her rejection has given her new direction. She has had the privilege to go into schools, churches, prisons and conferences to share her story of finding her acceptance and forgiveness through Christ. Like Chantel, we must somehow find the strength to mentally bundle all of our hostile feelings and surrender them to Christ.

After completing the five steps to forgiveness, pray this simple prayer:

_____

Lord, *I forgive (name of person) for (name the specifics). I refuse to give this offence any more of my time and any more of my emotional capacity. I give this area of my life back to the Lord Jesus Christ. I pray this in His name and in the power of His Holy Spirit. Amen.*

_____

This final part of the process is us untying the string to the mask of rejection and slowly pulling it away from our faces. Yes, it can be painful as we have worn the mask for so long, but the freedom and load that is lifted from our lives when we do this is invaluable to us walking out and living the life we have been called to live. Forgiveness doesn't make what they've done right, but it sets you free. The other person's behaviour and actions may never change; it's up to God, not us, to change others. Our responsibility is to be set free from the pressure and weight of an unforgiving attitude and the repercussions rejection has over our lives.

Whatever our pain or situation, we cannot afford to hold onto an unforgiving spirit. We must get involved in the process of releasing others from the debts we feel they owe us. If we keep our eyes on the One who forgave us, it will be a liberating force like nothing we've ever experienced. The mask will be lifted, and we will be able to see more clearly; we will have clarity of mind and a fresh confidence in our hearts, and we can run the race that's been mapped out for us. Whether it's with lycra and Vaseline or not, the words, insults and actions of others won't stop us finishing our course and winning our race!

Are you ready to remove another mask?

Heavenly Father, I give you the mask of rejection. I know you were rejected, and you understand my feelings of rejection. I choose to release them into your hands right now. Heal my heart, help me to move forward, and remove my focus from my past onto a glorious expectation for my future. In Jesus' name. Amen.

Chapter Three
– *Shame Unmasked*

'I WOULD HAVE. I could have, and I should have.' This is the soundtrack of shame. Underscored by a band of condemnation. The drums play 'you are not good enough for forgiveness', the bass line locks in with the drumbeat saying, 'you can never move past your pain'. The guitar riff strums over the top of the rhythm section, note after note, chord after chord, reminding you of everything you have ever done, before the lead singer, known as the devil sings: 'The devil knows your name, and calls you by your shame.' Is it any wonder, with the amps turned up so high, and the drums beating so loud, that it can feel impossible to take off the mask of shame? The soundtrack of shame has three characteristics that distinguish it from God's gentle grace-filled voice. Shame is always personal, pervasive and permanent.

If we were to run a diagnostic on the lead singer's voice, the first thing we would notice is: it is personal. The lyrics to our shame song are always focused on our past decisions, choices, regrets and mistakes. Shame never taunts you about someone else's shortcomings and failures. On the contrary, it's as if it's performing with you being the only person in the room. It is as if you have a front-row seat in a huge auditorium, and the band is performing for you only, and wanting to give you a performance you will never forget.

Shame is also pervasive, it doesn't just paralyse your potential; it impacts your present and future relationships. It causes a lack of conviction in our decisions and a lack of certainty in our identity. Shame doesn't just enter our ears when it sings, but it enters our hearts and minds with a tune that feels impossible to get out.

Shame is personal, it's pervasive, and it's permanent. It sings: 'You will always feel like this.' 'You will always carry that with you.' 'You can never tell anyone what you did.' It causes us to retreat into the shadows and to conceal who we are, layering our mask with more protective layers to make sure no one sees who we are or sees what we did.

I have been known to be a bit of an Apple groupie! iPhones, MacBook, iPods, you name it, and I've got it or think I need it. As a result, I can often be found at the Apple Genius Bar in one of their many stores. If rebooting my phone fails to fix the problem, I know where to turn for help. Thank God for Barry, my man at the Genius Bar! When my iPhone started misbehaving a while back, one of the geniuses told me there were two ways to reset my phone. Who knew? Evidently, just about everyone except me! A soft reset closes applications and clears your cache, but the data stored on your hard drive is not affected. That didn't do the trick, so we did a hard reset; it's also known as a factory reset because the iPhone is restored to the original manufacturer's settings it had when it left the factory floor. It reinitialises the core hardware components and reboots your operating system and all the settings, applications and data are wiped clean. It's a fresh start. It's a new phone.

You are probably thinking right now – Jon, why are you giving me a lesson in Apple diagnostics? I want to remind you that you, too, are a new creation! Not new as in Barry's soft reset (even though brother Barry's tender reset is a life saver), but new as in back to the beginning, new as in factory reset. It doesn't mean 'like new' it means 'brand new'. It's new in time, it's new in space and it's new in nature. It means perfect, pristine, mint condition right off the assembly line, latest and greatest. When you and I put our faith in Christ either for the first time or re-committing our lives to Him, it is a hard reset. It completely clears our history, as if it never happened. That's more than a phone device, and it's more than a paradigm shift—it's a factory reset.

At the cross, Jesus turned our regrets and 'if onlys' into complete certainties. He set us free, from condemnation and shame once and for all. We were set free, and the prison doors of past mistakes and future feelings of anxiety and despair broke wide open.

Shame received an eviction notice. It must give way to peace, certainty, assurance and security. However, this is not something that the majority of people experience in their day-to-day lives, or in their walk with Christ. Shame and security in Christ cannot coexist at the same time. They are not cousins, and they are not related; they are complete polar opposites. They cannot coexist with God's perfect love and affirmation of you as His chosen son or daughter. His love reboots our mindset, and heart, so that we can be fully alive, fully assured and fully accepted. One of my favourite verses in the Bible tells us that essentially God forgives and forgets. Really, Jon? Yes!

Hebrews 8:12 says: "God will remember our shortcomings and sins no more."

God is trying to remind us that our past is past. It is not supposed to weigh us down if we cast our cares upon God and give them to Him. Therefore, the question remains: why do so many people still listen to shame as the soundtrack of their lives? Why are so few people walking, living and enjoying the inheritance they have in Christ? Why aren't you fully alive and fully present in the now if He remembers everything you have done right, while forgetting what you have done wrong?

The enemy's soundtrack of shame is never going to stop playing unless we consciously decide and determine to change the track and tune in to a different frequency. God's grace doesn't clear the tracks that the devil creates, but it enables us to skip over them. When the enemy comes with shame and blame, we must train our brains to tell shame to go and measure the distance from east to west before attempting to come back, because that's how far your past sin is from the mind of God (Psalm 103). If you have confessed and addressed the part you had to play in the areas you feel shame, or if you have forgiven those that have caused you to feel a sense of shame, then you are learning to turn and move in the opposite direction that shame is luring you to walk in. We must remember that God never condemns us in order to shame us but always convicts us in order to change us. What we can get good at is learning how to better ignore the enemy's accusations, avoiding his song and approaching God's truth that He has spoken over us.

Like many, if not all of us, I made many mistakes growing up, and still to this day, the enemy tries to play his sound track of shame with lyrics like: "how can you lead a church with your past?" or "you don't deserve God's grace", and his other big one is "don't you feel like such a hypocrite?" Just because I'm a leader, pastor, a chaplain, it doesn't mean to say I don't feel such emotions. But the question remains: how do we unmask shame in our lives?

The answer is to shame the shamer as you confront the shame-based thinking. The first key as we mute the sound of shame in our lives is to recognise the areas where we are carrying shame, then shame the person that's singing the song of shame over our lives. If we do an audit of every area of our lives, we will see where the shamer sings. Imagine your life as a pie (I love pies), and each slice of the pie is an area of your life. Spiritual. Emotional. Relational. Vocational. Financial. Social. I guarantee any slice that you serve up will have the additive of shame intermingled into its taste because we don't think the ingredients of our personality, gift set and life will taste good when served up to others. 'You never save enough money'; therefore, your response to the song is to buy more to project the image of wealth and success. 'You are not as far ahead as you should be; therefore, you react by trying to climb the ladder of success by being someone that you are not. Whatever slice of your life pie is filled with shame, you can guarantee the chef is the accuser.

The Bible says there is a chef in the kitchen, "the accuser"

(Revelation 12:11), who tries to constantly add the ingredient of shame into every slice of our pie. The enemy constantly tries to accuse us by saying:

- You didn't read your Bible today
- You haven't prayed for a week
- You weren't nice to your spouse this morning
- You are a hypocrite and not really a Christian
- You could have done better at work this week
- You shouldn't have drunk so much at the party

To counter this, we have to be vulnerable with ourselves and own our story and shame the shamer with that vulnerability. I have noticed in our church that when one person leads with vulnerability many people follow. A common leadership axiom is people are impressed with your strength, but they are impacted by your vulnerabilities. I believe this is the truth when it comes to overcoming the insidious cycle of shame in our lives. As we let down our guard, we disarm the accuser because we break his power and hold over our lives. Ultimately, the devil is exposed when we expose our shame. An enemy exposed is an enemy on the way to defeat!

I vividly remember this to be the case when my dad passed away. Chantel and I were living in Cape Town, South Africa, and the enemy kept whispering, 'You didn't pray hard enough for him. You didn't have enough faith. Shame on you'. This caused me to feel a deep sense of inadequacy and guilt for many months. I felt a sense of condemnation that I was so busy with building the church and dealing with everyone else's challenges and problems, I wasn't there enough for my immediate family back in the UK. The question that was echoing in my ears for months after he passed was: 'Could I have been there more; could I have done something more to help?' After a journey of soul searching, I realised I had to make peace with myself. No one else was going to make me feel better, and no one else was going to be able to change the past. I had to own my decisions and choices, and I had to be vulnerable about how I felt. The accuser could not shame me anymore once I had owned my story and the part I had to play and acknowledged what I would do differently, accepting what Christ has done for me. We may all have our own story and journey with this uncomfortable mask, but the first step to removing the mask of shame is being honest about the past.

The enemy cannot wait for us to open our eyes in the morning; the first thing he wants to tell us is this:

You're not, you're not, you're not!

- You're not good enough to come to church
- You're not good enough to get that job
- You're not good enough to find a partner
- You're not good enough to get healed
- You're not good enough to be on a team at church

Recently, I had the opportunity to visit Israel. I was surrounded by incredible intellects, Bible scholars, Cambridge graduates and brilliant orators, and I found myself hearing the accuser say to me: 'You are not qualified. You're not in their league, you're not, you're not, you're not!' Instead of agreeing with the shamer, I realised I had to fight against it. As believers, we have to learn to strike back at the shamer and overpower the volume his voice speaks to us. So, when the accuser would try and shame me with 'you are not,' my response was:

"I am, I am, I am."

- I am the righteousness of God in Christ
- I am a new creation
- I am as a bold as a lion
- I am a child of God
- I am complete in Him
- I am alive with Christ
- I am free from the law of sin and death
- I am born of God
- I am more than a conqueror

We must learn to not just sit around and allow the enemy to tell us who we are not; we are to tell him who we are. Every time I say 'I am', I am declaring God's name and opinion of me over my shame and ultimately, over the shamer.

So, what else must we do? We must chase out shames attempts to creep back into our lives. We daily have to challenge his attacks and choose to chase him out. We can't leave behind things we fail to separate from. It has been said we need to give up to go up, and that is certainly the case with shame. We must loosen the accuser's grip on our lives, and every time it attempts to tag us back into the ring, we are to fight him off with faith and declarations. So often we let stumbling blocks become strongholds. That happens when we let negative thoughts or shame-based feelings dominate and occupy our focus. If you want to overcome an addiction, you have to shut it out of your life, not leave the door ajar. To put it another way, shame doesn't die easily, shame dies daily. Every day, when those feelings of shame coming knocking, you have to choose to shut them out. How do we do that? By submitting ourselves to God, resisting the enemy so he will flee from us. Allowing God to take our hand and relying upon His strength to shut the door of shame once and for all. As the enemy tries to push open the door to your heart and mind by singing, 'Shame on you', allow the power of God's Word and His presence to shout back: "Shame off you."

I often wonder why on earth does Chantel forgive me so often in our marriage, and when I say 'often' that's under played. She is so gracious. I still haven't worked out the toilet seat saga. If I leave it up, she gets frustrated because she has to put it down; and if I leave it down, she's unhappy, wondering why I didn't lift it up. I frustrate myself when the same habits and behaviour cause an argument or create tension; however, every single time she meets me with grace. Her desire for a relationship with me is stronger than my mistakes. How much more is God committed to forgiving us? It is His desire and delight in us that is the reason He chooses to forgive us, not any sense of duty or drudgery which shame suggests and screams. *'The steadfast love of the Lord never ceases; his mercies never come to an end; they are new every morning; great is your faithfulness.'* (Lamentations 3:22-23).

I would like to remind you that our shame dies when our story is told in safe places. As we begin to take off the mask of shame and unpeel the layers of regret and past failings, we become truly ourselves, but it must first happen in an environment of trust. Truth cannot be shared until trust is established. Therefore, we need to make sure we are not like the religious leaders in John Chapter 8, who appeared at a home and found a married women with another man. She was literally caught in the act of adultery, and they tried to publicly shame her, bringing her out into the public domain and preparing to stone her. Jesus challenged all of them, 'he that is without sin, to cast the first stone'. One by one, they dropped their stones and walked away. Jesus was left with this vulnerable woman, no doubt filled with shame and pain, and Jesus says, 'your sins are forgiven, go and sin no more!' The pharisees were committed to writing this woman off, whereas Jesus had another intention—to write her in to His story.

When stones are dropped from people's pockets, and hands are extended in love, that is when our shame can die, and we can really begin to live. Shame spreads and grows stronger when we internalise our defects and begin to infer that we are the only ones who struggle with the things that we struggle with. When this happens, we begin to sow fig leaves, like Adam and Eve did in the Garden of Eden, and we start to withdraw, compartmentalising our lives. As a consequence our true self fragments and lives in the shadows because we don't feel we can be accepted just as we are. We have a duty to make sure we don't cast out those that have made mistakes, we don't shipwreck and isolate those that are struggling, and we don't abandon those in need and who have hit some speed bumps and stumbling blocks on their journey.

The more Chantel and I journey through life as followers of Jesus the more we see the Christian life is like riding a bicycle, when one peddle is up the other peddle is down. The peddle that is up cannot boast to the peddle that is down because soon they will exchange places. So then, when I am up, I will pick you up, and when I am down, you will pick me up. Let us not be the only army on the earth that shoots its wounded. We are called to love people out of their shame and regret. We are to invite them home into the presence of a good, loving Father.

Of course, no two stories are the same, but we must remember our loving Father is the same, yesterday, today and forever. For us to be a community and a people that can lead people to take off the mask of shame, we need to focus on restoration. Our first impulse when something is broken is not to restore it, but to replace it. That's how I feel every time a piece of Apple equipment stops working or doesn't operate how I would like it to. But that attitude cannot work with people. We need to cultivate a community and environment where people feel safe to take off the mask of shame and be accepted just as they are. Perhaps you are preparing to take off the mask of shame for the first time. If so, let me remind you that shame is nothing more than a bully that can never push past the shield that is grace and truth. My dad taught me that at school you must always stand up to a bully, and it's the same with shame you have to hit it head on. You are safely protected and guarded behind the defence of Jesus. You are embraced and shielded by His love, so the shrapnel of shame cannot get near you nor harm you because Jesus Christ accepts you.

I would like to end this chapter by giving you a vivid picture of what Jesus does with our shame. There was a father who decided to make his son, Billy, a video; it was a highlight reel of his football career, the best moments of his short career. On the day of Billy's birthday the father played the video he edited and prepared for Billy, and Billy sat down and began to watch it. Clip after clip, the son watched the goals fly in, from an overhead scissors kick to dribbling round the opposing team before placing the ball in the corner. You would think he was Messi or Ronaldo! As the last scene played, Billy sat back and after a deep breathe said to his dad: 'Wow, that was amazing. Was I really that good?' What Billy hadn't realised was that his dad had made him look better than he really was. Billy's dad deleted the missed penalties (sounds like me in my prime), the foul play, the sending off's, the yellow cards the poor tackles, and cut them onto the editing room floor, so all Billy was left with were his best moments.

That is exactly what our Heavenly Father has done for us. As we address our shame and commit to taking off the mask by sharing our story with trusted people and in safe places, God edits and slices and dices, working all our life together for the good, and all the fouls, missed shots and mistakes get edited out of the video and don't make the final cut. God, the master editor, adds in our righteousness instead of the red card. He covers our kit in His grace when it should be mud and dirt. God takes our entire lives and all the shame we feel and writes His own story over the top of it, editing out those pieces that we turned away from, yet editing in all the benefits we have in Christ, and places them upon us. That is the truth of the gospel everything we are not, we become when we put our faith in Christ and as we peel off the mask of shame, we become who we were always made to be. Stop remembering what God has forgotten. Today is a new day; your past is gone, and you are a new creation in Christ.

To help remind you of who you are in Christ, and to tune out the soundtrack of shame in your life, here are some declarations to speak over yourself and your life on a daily basis. You can put them on your desk at work, or on your mirror in the bathroom, or on your bedside table. Speak these words in faith, and silence the sound of shame!

- I am the righteousness of God in Christ
- I am a new creation
- I am as a bold as a lion
- I am a child of God
- I am complete in Him
- I am alive with Christ
- I am free from the law of sin and death
- I am born of God
- I am, I am, I am!

When you put on these truths on a daily basis, you will be able to take off the mask of shame, once and for all!

Heavenly Father, I take off the mask of shame because you have taken my shame on yourself. At the cross, you set me free, you called me your own, and I no longer walk under the weight of feeling 'not good enough', but I stand enough in your Presence, because you paid the price for my shame. Amen.

Chapter Four
– *Guilt Unmasked*

I WILL never forget the moment a few years ago when we were living in Cape Town, South Africa. We were in 'Pick 'n' Pay' the local supermarket (my wife picked, I paid). Chantel is the most friendly, warm, endearing person on the planet. She talks to anyone and everyone and always leaves them feeling better...apart from the dear lady in the supermarket that day. She gets chatting to her and says with the uttermost sincerity, whilst tapping her on the tummy: "How many weeks are you now?" In that moment, the lady says something which left Chantel in the deepest hole imaginable: "I'm not pregnant." As she said it, I walked away and all I could hear was my poor wife saying: "I am so sorry." There was no way back from that one. It certainly goes down as one of Chantel's most embarrassing moments, and she won't want to be playing that back in her mind too often. For the next few days, Chantel lived with this mask of guilt as she played the clip back in her head, as if on repeat, over and over again. Guilt hits us all in different ways. As a dad, a pastor, a chaplain and a friend, one of my areas where I constantly feel guilty is where I spend my time. When I'm at work, I feel like I'm cheating my family; when I'm at home, I feel I should be doing more at work, and I can continually live with this mask of guilt. Juggling competing demands causes me to be prone to feeling guilty on a regular basis and often regret as well.

As a pastor of a relatively young demographic, I have seen and heard my fair share of horror stories of trips to tattoo parlours that went drastically wrong. I think there is a reason people say: 'Think before you ink!' When I hear such stories, I think to myself, 'I'd love them to FaceTime me in so they can hear me say to them: 'Do you really need to carry your girlfriend's name on your arm for the rest of your life when you have only been dating a month?' There is no 'undo' key once the needle starts to paint on your body! Many of us have had those moments in our lives. This could be why the television series 'Tattoo Fixers' has been so pop-ular. Viewers follow the story of choices that turn into regret, as individuals regret the tattoo they received and ask for a talented tattoo artist to remove it or cover it up. Tattooists are renowned for removing mistakes, they are experts at cover-ups. At an af-fordable rate, they can get the ink out of your skin. Is it going to sting? Yes. Is it going to be uncomfortable? Most certainly. But it will remove the unwanted signs and symbols from your past. I mean who wouldn't want to remove 'I love Barbara' from their thigh? Or 'Barry Balls forever' from their buttock?

It may not be tattoos, but I am quite confident in asserting that you have regrets. It might not be a symbol reminding you of an ink souvenir you picked up on a lad's holiday, but you have the memories of something. You did not embed his name onto your arm, but you feel regret and guilt over words left said or deeds done. Guilt tends to leave its own tattoo of sorts inked into our minds and hearts and leaves a permanent stain in our lives. It has been said that reflection turns experience into insight, so a few years ago, I decided to do an inventory of sorts. I asked myself a series of questions, important questions at that, as to how I was really doing. As I reflected, I asked myself a challenging question: If there were any unaddressed, unidentified or unresolved guilt issues that manifest in the form of a tattoo, how many marks would I have? What images of pain, brokenness and regret would appear in front of me? I wonder how you would answer that question? Perhaps an experience you wish you had never taken part in. An argument that you left unresolved. A person that you betrayed. If we reflect and ponder long enough, we would all find seasons of selfishness, wasted opportunities, anger, shortcuts and unnecessary consequences.

I recently read the 14 reasons we feel guilty:

1. Giving in to a craving
2. Not calling family & friends often enough
3. Not sticking to your healthy eating plan
4. Not going to the gym
5. Leaving a pet at home
6. Hitting your snooze button
7. Not recycling
8. Booking a holiday on your credit card
9. Not finishing a book (this was me for two years)
10. Checking emails while you read with your children
11. Unfollowing someone on social media
12. Not using your juicer
13. Hiding your online shopping delivery before your spouse gets home
14. Exchanging unwanted Christmas gifts

Clearly guilt is nothing new! Most people wrestle with guilt; it's defined as a feeling of responsibility or remorse for some offence, crime or wrongdoing, whether real, exaggerated or imagined. In other words, guilt has two insidious components: The actual offence and the feelings that accompany it. When we have unaddressed guilt in our lives, it bleeds into every area of our being. Guilt is defined as 'an *emotional state that comes when we feel we have failed to live up to our own or other people's morals or standards*.' Guilt keeps us focused on the times we've failed and is outworked through distressing emotions like sadness, anger or anxiety. It can even cause physical reactions such as an upset stomach. We've all heard it said 'I feel sick to my stomach'—so often guilt causes not just emotional turmoil but physical challenges. I think guilt is ingrained somewhere in our human experience; we've all made mistakes, put our foot in it, said something we regret or done something we are ashamed of, and we're left with this overwhelming feeling of guilt.

Guilt triggers a number of emotions in our lives, and often the first emotion it triggers is a sense of self-protection. When we try to protect ourselves, we hide our guilt by compartmentalising it or completely hiding it from others, we are not vulnerable, open or transparent. Instead, we limit our lives to simply suppressing the secret and tearing down any image that does not line up with the image we want to project. Guilt can lie festering and untreated. This can cause our lives to build walls without windows—walls that keep people out as opposed to windows that let good things come in and bad things go out.

Secondly, it triggers the emotion of self-defeat. We define ourselves by what we did and the consequences and impact of whom we have hurt. We take ownership of what we did so much so that we let what we did own us. We adopt it, and it becomes our identity. We adapt our behaviour to be focused on externals and keeping a positive reputation. The irony of attempting to hide our guilt is we wear it on our arms and react to life through the filter of our past regrets, mistakes and failures.

The third emotion guilt triggers is self-condemnation. Despite us being told in the Bible that God cleans us up, washes out our sin and makes us brand new, we tend to wear our past as the only hoodie or jacket we own. We must remember God specialises in removing our past failures and our guilt. He can take out every last stain, extracting every thread that's been scoured or scourged by sin. In fact, if you believe in Jesus, you have endless grace, washing you clean and making you whole. Grace is a gift. It cannot be earned. It is undeserved and unmerited favour. We who are often burdened us down, because of the guilt that we unnecessarily carry around with us (Matthew 11:28). Whatever your dosage of guilt and shame, Jesus wants to say to you today it is too much. Recognise the guilt, regulate your thoughts that trigger guilt, and respond with the reality that you are saved by grace, you are shielded by grace and you are sanctified (a big church word that simply means in the process of becoming more like Jesus).

I have just identified the guilt we feel in our past, but what about the guilt we often feel in the present? Virtually every religion and every therapist has had to come up with a way to deal with the universal experience of guilt. Now, there are some people who have an over-active guilt meter. There are people who feel guilty about everything, even things that the vast majority of us would not regard as being close to being wrong. These hyper-sensitive, guilt-prone people remind me of a defective smoke alarm that goes off when you light a candle in your house or cook something on the stove. Several times a day there is this shrill, high-pitched alarm that sets everyone on edge and makes everyone in the house continually irritable and agitated. I think of lots of folks feel guilty because they are not meeting some absolutely unrealistic standard imposed upon them by others. Whether it's guilt from the past or the present, if we carry it around long enough, it becomes an unnecessary burden and weight. Guilt is the corrosion of the soul, and it can only be dissolved in the blood of Jesus.

I love the story of a man who entered a bar, bought a glass of beer and then immediately threw it into the bartender's face. Quickly grabbing a napkin, he helped the bartender dry his face while he apologised with great remorse. "I'm so sorry," he said. "I have this compulsion to do this. I fight it, but I don't know what to do about it." "You had better do something about your problem," the bartender replied. "You can be sure I will remember you and will never serve you another drink until you get help." It was months later the man faced the bartender again. When he asked for a beer, the bartender refused. Then the man explained that he had been seeing a psychiatrist and that his problem was solved. Convinced it was now okay to serve him, the bartender poured him a drink. The man took the glass and splashed the beer into the bartender astonished face. "I thought you were cured," the shocked bartender screamed. "I am," said the man. "I still do it, but I don't feel guilty about it anymore."

As funny as that story is, some of us have become numb to our guilt. We wear a mask of indifference. On the one hand, we are carrying too much guilt around with us; on the other, we have no sense of guilt or conscious because we have been anaesthetised and given permission to never feel bad about what we have done. What is a healthy balance? What should we believe? How should we respond and ultimately take the mask of guilt off in our lives? We must remember that guilt is not a new meme that you can find on your iPhone, it's been around since the very first moments of humanity. It was guilt that caused Adam and Eve to hide when God came walking in the cool of the day and to wear fig leaves to cover their naked bodies (Genesis 3:7). It was guilt over his adulterous affair that caused King David to say, *'When I kept silent, my bones wasted* away from my groaning all day long." (Psalm 32:1). It was guilt that caused Isaiah to cry out 'Woe is me for I am a man with unclean lips' (Isaiah 6:5) when he came into the presence of the Living God.

When the Pharisees brought the woman caught in adultery, Jesus looked at the angry mob and said, *"If any one of you is without sin, let him be the first to through a stone at her."* (John 8:7). It was guilt that caused the men to drop their stones, one by one, and walk away. Guilt is not God's design and certainly not our best life, so what is the solution for guilt?

In the good old days growing up, we used to make tree houses. Nowadays, children download apps and play Call of Duty or Fortnite. However, rather than our fingers getting warn out from tapping console controllers, we used to come home with splinters. Sometimes I would get really deep splinters, and I just left them, rather than trying to pull them out because it would be too uncomfortable. A splinter is a tiny piece of the past which has the potential to cause havoc in the future. Left in, a splinter can have fatal consequences starting with an infection called tetanus which can result in death. Guilt is like a splinter because it goes in deep, then it is hidden away but over time it causes serious infection, impacting every area of our lives. The healing in my finger from the splinter could not begin until the splinter was pulled out. Similarly, the cross our Saviour was crucified on wasn't a smooth, varnished, well-finished cross like we see in the shops; this was two pieces of rugged wood full of splinters. The cross would have splintered Jesus' back, his feet and his hands. Every splinter which Jesus took on the cross was for our guilt. You don't have to carry guilt because Jesus took it on your behalf. It is at the cross that a divine exchange takes place. He says, 'Give me your guilt, and I will exchange it with my grace'. To put it another way: When the splinter of guilt went in, the blood of grace came out.

It is generally recognised and understood that Psalm 51 is the most relevant and informative passage on guilt and how to deal with it. It is written by a man by the name David. When you parachute into a Bible passage, you can often miss the context of what has happened when it was written. So, to fill you in, David had just committed adultery with a woman named Bathsheba. She was married to one of his military men, Uriah. One day, after their romantic encounter, Bathsheba approached David to tell him that she was pregnant, ouch! David's response, instead of heading to IKEA to buy a cot and decorate the nursery, was to panic, and he desired to cover up the incident. However, there was one problem. Bathsheba's husband had been fighting in the battlefields for months on end; therefore, there was no way that Bathsheba's child could be Uriah's. So, David organised for him to be put on the frontlines of battle so that he would be killed by the opposing army. When this happened, David was exposed to the consequences of his actions by a man named Nathan, and David writes Psalm 51 in a moment of self-discovery. David spirals into a pit of despair and a dungeon of guilt deeper than any physical dungeon he could experience. He was in the spiritual and emotional depths, and yet this psalm says that he got out of his guilt. We can only imagine how he felt—the guilt, the shame, the horror, the self-hatred—after infidelity, indirect murder and the intention to hurt a man fighting for his own kingdom.

How did David take off the mask of guilt? He drew a distinction between repentance and remorse. Remorse is the sadness that you have for been caught whereas repentance, (which means a change of thinking, and setting a new course) is a genuine sadness that we have fallen short of God's standards and have a genuine desire to change. David said:

> *"Be gracious to me, O God, according to*
> *Your lovingkindness; according to the greatness*
> *of Your compassion blot out my transgressions.*
> *Wash me thoroughly from my iniquity and cleanse*
> *me from my sin." (Psalm 51:1-2).*

In the rest of the Psalm, David really gets into it. You can feel his desperation to move on from his sin and be restored to right standing with God. When I fall short, I want to be like David and realise what my sin cost Jesus on the cross but be confident in the fact that I can be forgiven when I am genuinely sorry for my actions. We can then be given a clean slate! If you want a clean slate, I believe the following four tips can help you take off the mask of guilt.

First, take ownership of your story. As long as you find a reason to reject taking responsibility for yourself and continue shifting the blame onto others for whatever is missing or has been robbed in your life, you will focus on what's wrong rather than what can be made right. This delays our healing and causes us to take a 'detour' that prolongs us from reaching our destination. Even if your guilt runs deep, it is essential that you learn to forgive yourself and anyone associated with the guilt you feel.

The apostle Paul was a murderer of Christians. Previously called Saul, he was a religious zealot, a hypocrite and an aggressive threat to the early Church. Then, on the road to Damascus, as he prepared to kill and take more Christians captive, God met him, struck him down off his horse, and introduced Himself to Saul. Saul had a dramatic conversion and gave the rest of his life to converting non-Christians and establishing churches all over Europe and Asia Minor. That's why Paul's words in Colossians 3:12-13 carry so much weight:

"Bear with each other and forgive one another
if any of you has a grievance against someone.
Forgive as the Lord forgave you."
COLOSSIANS 3:12-13:

Second, be honest with yourself. We can't deny the reality of our situation nor ignore the truth of what we are feeling. Our tendency is often to try to ignore our past or bury any sign of its existence. However, if you don't come face to face with God and hear what He wants to reveal within your own heart, you will continue to be entrapped by guilt and suffer the needless harmful effects of such damaging emotions.

Third, I think it is helpful to ask Jesus to heal the broken places in your life. Jeremiah 17:14 says: 'Heal me, Lord, and I will be healed; save me and I will be saved, for you are the one I praise.' We should specifically name the different areas of our lives where we feel guilt and begin to confess any sinful responses to such emotions. We can then choose to cooperate with God's healing process. The Spirit will restore and transform you into Christ's image as you surrender to His authority. This is not easy to do, but it is necessary when trying to overcome feelings of guilt.

Fourth, don't keep secrets. In our family, one of our core values is we don't keep secrets from each other. Outside of Christmas and fun surprises like gifts and holidays, we do everything we can not to keep secrets from one another. Like all young people growing up, Chantel and I both made our fair share of mistakes in relationships, friendships, with our money—the list goes on. Once we made a life-long commitment to one another 15 years ago, we decided that the only way to conduct a healthy relationship and friendship for the next 50+ years (she honestly can't get enough of me) was to talk about our past and our mistakes. Those conversations weren't easy, but the reality is now we can live in complete freedom; we certainly don't have a perfect marriage, but it is healthy. We encourage our children to be open and honest with us even when the truth hurts. It's a lot easier to keep secrets in the short term, but in the long term it becomes a lot harder, and those secrets soon turn to guilt. Wherever there's secrets, there are always guilt.

Of course, this is not always easy, but we can escape the guilt trap as we train our brains to believe God's truth instead of focusing on our feelings. If you still feel guilty after confessing your wrongdoings, you know that your feelings are not syncing with

God's Word. I often find it useful to find Bible verses that remind me that I am forgiven, and I am righteous because Jesus died on the cross for me. I write them down in a short list and then read through the encouraging verses and reflect on what they mean for me and my life. When I do this, my emotions eventually catch up with my thoughts, and I become free from the feelings of guilt. As a Christian, I believe that Jesus' death made a way for you and me to be completely free from guilt but also the feelings that accompany it. This helps me 'drop' guilt as a constant companion.

A few people reading this might be tempted to dismiss this chapter because you feel as though you have made too many mistakes (you're in very good company), had too many failures, taken too many steps back, and you wonder: "If I messed up again, is there really hope for me?" I think that's the power of the good news that Christians believe. There is a God who can't take His eyes off of you. And until you understand the Father's love for you and that He loves you when you least expect it and least deserve it, it's hard to have hope. Christianity isn't behaviour modification to train you to be a good person; it's complete transformation. Jesus came to re-condition our reflexes. We all too easily strengthen our guilt reflex when the gospel is about God reconditioning every reflex in our body, and that includes the reflexes we have towards ourselves, so when we look in the mirror we don't see guilt and failures, but we see the righteousness of Christ.

Lamentations 3:23 is one of the most beautiful promises in Scripture. *"His mercies are new every morning."* I've been thinking about, meditating on and studying this verse, and I've discovered something I hadn't noticed before. The word 'new' doesn't just mean again and again and again. It means different. Did you sin the same way today as you did yesterday or the day before? Or was it different? And is it possible that God's mercy is different today than it was yesterday or the day before? I don't think there is a single day that goes by when there isn't some sinful thought or action, or something in my life, that I need to confess to the Lord. His mercy hits the reset button in our lives, and He can do that today!

I don't know if you have come across a recent social phenomenon called 'ghosting'? Ghosting has been described as the practice of ending a personal relationship with someone by suddenly, and without explanation, withdrawing from all communication. That's what we need to do when feelings of guilt surface within us. We cannot accommodate or entertain them; we don't enter into conversation with them, nor engage with them. Instead, we turn our backs and start a conversation with God in His Word. Next time you feel a sense of guilt, I want you to go through this checklist so you can expose and identify guilt for what it is, a lie that the enemy wants you to wear:

- Beating yourself up and wrestling yourself to the ground for past choices, mistakes and imperfections
- Feeling as though you can never do enough and will never be enough
- Saying "yes" when the best answer is "no"
- Letting others guilt-trip you
- Allowing others to repeatedly overstep boundaries and take advantage of you
- Going along with dysfunctional cyclical behaviour as though it's normal
- Not speaking up when you need and want to because you fear people's rejection of you

As we come to the end of this chapter, it is worth us doing an audit of how you are doing in terms of wearing or taking off the mask of guilt. If we were to go to the hospital, they would take an X-ray of your interior life – what would it reveal? Regret over a bad decision? Guilt about the temptation you didn't resist? Guilt is always hidden beneath the external behaviours, and it festers, irritates and agitates us. If you want an extraction, if you're clogged up and need some help, we have learned that there is a way out, and we can have an extraction! We confess. Plain and simple, ask God to help you. Psalm 139:23-24 is a model prayer: 'Search me, O God, and know my heart; try me, and know my anxieties; and see if there is any wicked way in me, and lead me in the way everlasting.' When we confess, we find a freedom that others don't. He promised to forgive you, and that is what He will do. Not maybe, not I could do, not I would do or even I should do, but I will forgive you!

When a friend of mine's son was young, he approached his dad with a confession. 'Daddy, I took a crayon and drew on the wall.' My friend sat his son down and tried to be wise by saying, "Was that the smartest thing to do in the house?" He replied, "No." The father said: "What do you think Daddy should do when you write on the wall?" "Tell me off" His son said. "What do you think Daddy should do this time?" "I think you should love", the boy replied. Don't we all long for that? Don't we all want a father who even though our guilt and mistakes are before us, written all over the wall, will choose to love us anyway? Don't we all long for and want a father who cares for us and loves us in spite of our mistakes?

The good news is, we do have that type of father. A Father who shows us His best when we are at our very worst. A Father whose grace for us is strongest when our faithfulness is at its weakest. If your guilt jar is full, then you can end this chapter with some great news: Your guilt is no more, it has been taken, and you have a Father that loves you.

Father, thank you so much for your amazing grace that covers every bad deed I have done and every word I have spoken. I do not need to wallow in any feelings of guilt because I am free. So, remind me to turn to you and focus on the truth of your Word instead of focusing on my feelings and emotions. I pray this in Jesus' name! Amen.

Chapter Five
– *Perfectionism Unmasked*

A MAN once approached the famous British preacher C.H. Spurgeon at a Christian retreat centre and said in a very pious but confident tone of voice that he had reached a state of spiritual perfection. Without a word, Spurgeon picked up a jug of ice cold water and poured it on the man's head. When the man became angry and swore and shouted (reacting like any normal person would if cold water was poured on his head), Spurgeon said, "Well, now I know exactly what spiritual perfection you've come to!"

All joking aside, by my very nature and personality, I am probably what is known as a perfectionist. Whether it's when my family and I go on holidays, or I step into a restaurant, Sunday church service, or even when I'm watching a boxset on Netflix at home, my expectation is one of 'this better be good this better be perfect'. I want a perfect experience, without hiccups or hang-ups, but I've come to realise that is not how life works. The challenge with this mindset is, very rarely (if ever) are my expectations met, and often the very high standards of expectation I put on others, I place on myself. This leads to high levels of frustration and what I call 'destination disease.' "One day things will be better." "Next time my team will meet my standards." "The next meal out will be the perfect meal out". The old adage rings true: "the perfect is the enemy of the good." Recently, productivity experts have put a twist on it to emphasise the consequence: "the perfect is the enemy of the done." If you are anything like me, you can all too easily miss a good experience, lose contentment or forfeit a significant moment or memory because of the frustration in pursuing perfection.

The Christmas season often highlights the mask of perfections in our lives. We build Christmas up to be something which it rarely lives up to in reality. The family all home, content and getting along, snow falling, the fire burning and Christmas dinner looking like something from the front of one of Delia Smith's cookbooks (let's be havin' you). But more often than not, it doesn't snow, the family is squabbling and the turkey isn't cooked properly. We feel disappointed, let down and frustrated. Perfectionism magnifies your mistakes and minimises your progress.

I am a big believer that we should endeavour to try our very best and strive for excellence in all that we do, but there is a very fine line when this desire becomes detrimental to our peace, satisfaction and life fulfilment. If you wonder whether you are a 'perfectionist' or have 'perfectionist tendencies', do any of the following characteristics and traits describe you?

- You take on new tasks and responsibilities even if your plate is already full because you know you could do it better than somebody else
- You find it hard to delegate and eliminate because you want to make progress, but you want it to be perfect
- You tend to worry a lot and are anxious about every little detail because you need to feel and be in control
- You focus intensely on completing tasks, which makes you feel good about yourself
- You often focus on other people and try to control the narrative because you don't want to display weakness or vulnerability

Don't worry if you said yes to one or more, or even all of these, as I wrote them all about me. You see, this is a mask I continually struggle to remove.

The sad reality of perfectionism is that it is never finished. That's the lie it sells us. There's no such thing as perfect; you can always improve. So, perfectionism draws an ever moving, ever expanding finish line that you never reach. For Christians, spiritual perfectionism is a pervasive and insidious problem. It's danger-ous precisely because so many of us mistake it for a spiritual vir-tue. Spiritual perfectionism is that same obsession with control and flawlessness transposed into our relationship with God. It's rooted in the lie that we can earn God's love and perform our way towards God's affections. Most of us know better than to think that out loud, and yet we often live like we believe it.

The Bible calls us to excellence, not perfectionism. Perfec-tionism is often confused with excellence and even perfection itself, but it is neither, although sometimes the lines can blur. Ex-cellence is a determination to do something as well as possible with the resources and time on hand. Perfectionism, on the oth-er hand, is rooted in pride and is often a fear-based compulsion which can result in us getting hurt or hurting those around us. Perfectionism has the potential to wreak havoc in our lives if we don't recognise and address it. Edwin Bliss said, "The pursuit of excellence is gratifying and healthy. The pursuit of perfection is frustrating, neurotic, and a terrible waste of time." One of the rea-sons this book took so long to write was I was wearing the mask of perfectionism; I want it to be perfect, but there's no such thing as perfect. This book is ME, which is far from perfect. I had to go on a journey of realising that it will never be perfect, but it will be my best. Best is always better than perfect.

Perfectionism nearly always has its roots in our desire for ac-ceptance and our fear of rejection. There it is, that word again: RE-JECTION. We strive, try and toil for perfection so hard in order to prove ourselves to others so that we don't experience rejection. The biggest lie of perfectionism is "the harder I work to achieve perfection, the more I will feel accepted." Perfectionism can also be fuelled by comparison. Do you know why other people's lives often look so attractive? It's because they only show us the good bits and their highlight reel. We compare our lives to somebody else's, not understanding the context of their story! Comparison breeds jealousy and envy and causes us to rot from the inside out. No one puts a bad hair day, a big zit on your nose, screaming kids or dirty laundry on social media; we put on our best.

When was the last time I instagrammed empty seats in church (there's been plenty of those during the lockdowns), miserable worshippers with their hands in their pockets or unhappy kids in Kids Church? No! We show the world our best even though it's never a true reflection of reality.

We perform in order to be validated, verified and vindicated. The desire is for others to see us and approve us, which is completely the opposite of God's desire for us. We walk into church in our Sunday best, with a big smile. Therefore, we are driven to perfection by trying to keep up with everyone else's so called 'perfect life', when in reality, their lives are pretty much the same as ours—real! Pain, problems, pandemics and predicaments will define our life on Earth, and no one can escape it or be exempt from such a reality. A key truth that we need to grapple with and get our heads round' is that nowhere in the Bible does it encourage us to try and be perfect, quite the contrary. The good news is Jesus perfectly lived, died and rose again for us. He has already purchased our perfection. We can live in His freedom. Perfection isn't earned but received we are perfect in Christ. God the Father sees us as perfectly righteous in Christ we are perfect because we are joined together with Christ in faith. Jesus Himself, is the author and finisher of our faith.

God is calling us to refocus our eyes away from ourselves and how we're measuring up, and fixing them onto Jesus instead because perfectionism is a mask we must lay aside in the race of faith. Instead of being obsessed with focusing on perfection and creating the perfect avatar for others, we can focus on Christ's perfect love for us. I believe that there are three issues that can often arise in our faith walk make our lives particularly suscepti-ble to perfectionism.

The first is our struggle with a sense of inadequacy for the call-ing and assignment placed on our lives. This isn't a question of competency but something that runs with much deeper roots; it's a genuine sense of unworthiness to carry the responsibility of what we have been called to do. We feel inadequate and un-qualified, forgetting that actually no one is qualified because God equips the called, as opposed to calling the equipped. Every-thing we have is a result of God's limitless grace, and so we should have an assurance and courage that whatever we are called to do, wherever we are, we can remain confident that the outcome is God's responsibility, but obedience is ours.

Issues of perfectionism begin to take hold in our lives when we sense the need to prove our value through living a perfor-mance-oriented existence as opposed to a position-oriented existence in our leadership. A 'self-proving' lifestyle sets us up for a neverending cycle of activity, measured against an impos-sible benchmark of our own standards. The whole of the Bible is telling a story about how humanity's best efforts were never good enough, and it took a perfect person in the form of Jesus to come and do what we could never do for ourselves. Jesus is our marker, our measurement and metric system for success be-cause if we weigh our worth and ability against our own stan-dards, we discover there is no marker for the point at which we have 'done enough'. Our lives have no parameters to contain our activity and over-sacrifice; grind and hustle have become univer-sally celebrated. Every target, every performance and every ac-complishment, to a perfectionist should and must be bettered year upon year. We end up focusing on goals and outcomes as opposed to growth and the journey. One way we can overcome this is through exploring our own drive to achieve and addressing the root of why we want everything to be perfect.

The second issue perfectionism creates is unrealistic expectations and projections onto others that spoil their experiences and our own. I regularly have to do an audit of my life and see how I am doing on the 'perfectionism barometer'. The more affirmation I need, the harder it is for me to lead, and perfectionism becomes like a poison that slowly, subtly and surely corrodes my passion, confidence and belief in myself which flows out towards others. This can cause us to push people too hard, which creates burn out and exhaustion because of endless activity and 'sacrifice' for the mission. Many type A leaders will be able to relate to this.

So many times I have come home from church after what 99% of people would have said was an unforgettable time in God's house, yet I cannot seem to forget the one moment which didn't live up to the high standards I have set for myself and others. It can even be as small as the words didn't come up in time on the screen, or someone forgot to set the heating correctly. My frustrations can bubble over and cause me to forget all the incredible moments which took place, including people making their peace with God.

At an greater extreme, if you are bent towards wearing the mask of perfectionism, you will often give regular feedback that can be critical and at times unrealistic. Yes, we should always seek to improve and better ourselves, but often 'speaking the truth' takes precedence over 'speaking the truth in love'. This helps us to protect ourselves from our own self-scrutiny by projecting it onto other people's weaknesses, shortcomings and misdemeanours. If left unchecked, the damage this creates is very real and serious for relationships.

Finally, I believe that the third vulnerability to perfectionism we carry is in our strength of desire to truly belong and be accepted for who we are. We all have emotional needs and we want to feel accepted for who we are, not for what we do. When we try to live perfect lives, we live as though others are holding up scorecards every time we speak, operate in our gifts, or every time we initiate something. This can leave us vulnerable to putting our peace, contentment and joy in other people's hands. In my experience as a pastor and a chaplain, I have noticed that perfectionism can generate a fear of exclusion. Our fears of being judged by others or not measuring up leads us to be more critical of ourselves and others. Instead of fostering security and belonging, it stifles creativity, sharpens our awareness of other people's opinions and solidifies the lies we tell ourselves about us. To put it another way, our vulnerabilities become scars to hide behind, as opposed to stories to share. This mask that we wear not only threatens the social fabric in which perfectionism runs rife, but also, if left undetected and unaddressed, is projected onto our view of God.

So how do you take off the mask of perfectionism once and for all? I find it very helpful, as a person whose prone to perfectionism, to sit in Matthew 11:28-30, which is an invitation of sorts to those of us who are worn out by religion and performance-based living—which is, of course, our perfectionistic nature. Jesus says: *'Are you tired? Worn out? Burned out on religion? Come to me. Get away with me and you'll recover your life. I'll show you how to take a real rest. Walk with me and work with me—watch how I do it. Learn the unforced rhythms of grace. I won't lay anything heavy or ill-fitting on you. Keep company with me and you'll learn to live freely and lightly.'*

In these three verses alone, we find the cure for our perfectionist tendencies: Walk with God, this is about presence. Work with God, this is about partnership. Watch with God, this is about perspective. I believe these three keys unlock the door to the prison cell that perfectionism puts us in and frees us from a performance-based mindset and lifestyle. All three of these things, walking, working and watching are a result of God's grace towards us. Before we ever initiated anything for Him, He already established His love for us. It is dancing to the rhythms of grace as opposed to the perfectionistic voice of inferiority and inadequacy that wills you to play a role that you pretend to be, so that others will think you are acceptable to them and to God. God is calling us to the wonderfully refreshing experience of getting our eyes off ourselves and how we're measuring up and onto Jesus. He wants us to stop pursuing or being paralysed by perfectionism so we are free to pursue love and pursue trusting Him alone with every fibre of our being.

In Christ, you are free! You are free to follow Jesus imperfectly. You are free to fight the fight of faith defectively because that's the only way you will remove the mask of perfection—by walking, working and watching with Jesus. Let's unpack each of these three elements in turn.

When we walk with Jesus, we are keeping pace with Jesus we are not trying to go ahead of God and impose our deadlines on God's timeline. On the contrary, when we walk with Jesus we are in step with Him—close enough to hear His voice, near enough to obey His commands. We are not too far ahead of God, striving to do things in our own strength, and we are not far behind God, acting lazy or slothful. It's a balance of hearing God speak, actively listening and then intentionally moving when He speaks. This is the starting point to us working with God and partnering with Him.

WORK WITH JESUS

When we work with Jesus, we work as friends, not servants. Therefore, we know that if we do our best, prepare well and work to the best of our ability, God will be able to say to us 'well done my good and faithful servant.' God wants to see you partner with Him knowing you work like it depends on you but praying like it depends on God. This helps us deal with our perfectionism because we know without Christ, even our best efforts will come up short. But when we work with Jesus, He provides for us and gives us His power.

WATCHING WITH JESUS

Lastly, we are to watch Jesus. We are to watch how He lived. The Bible is full of encounters when Jesus meets someone in their sin, weakness or vulnerability and rather than expose them, embraces them with His lovingkindness. That may seem a bit soppy and touchy feely for our liking, but Jesus didn't expose people's weaknesses He covered them by His strength. When we see the way Jesus dealt with people's imperfections, we will be inspired and instructed not to be too harsh on others or impose our standards of perfection onto their experiences, and we can imitate the life that was modelled to us in the pages of the Bible.

I really believe that perfectionism is the enemy of spiritual growth. It makes it harder for us to rest in Christ's love and causes us to relentlessly work to make sure we achieve to receive. God says rest, and you can receive my love, not race towards fulfilling a goal, a target, or the end of quarter results. Of course, the bottom-line matters, and we want to be prosperous, fruitful and successful, but what good is it to gain all those things and lose ourselves in the process? More often than not, when perfectionists reach their desired destination, they are not satisfied when they get there because they always think they could have got there in a more efficient and effective way. The only perfection we need to rejoice in is the perfect love of Jesus. We can be joyful in our imperfect state and set free by perfect love Himself.

One of the things (and there are many, including getting to watch the greatest team on Earth, the Canaries) I love about living in Norfolk is the amount of countryside, the beautiful views we get to enjoy from close to our home. We get a stunning view from our driveway when the sun rises and falls. That all changes, however, when the British weather kicks in. There is often just enough rain to completely obstruct the view from our bedroom. In a similar way, our perfectionism may be responsible for obstructing the image of our perfect Father in Heaven, that is impeding our view and imposing dark rain clouds above our homes. Each of us has a picture of who God our Father is like. Often, our view of a perfect God is obstructed by the experience we have had of our imperfect earthly fathers. We can't accept our Heavenly Father because of earthly memories.

The reality is He is loving and inclusive, whereas perfectionism is imposing and obstructing. Perfectionism is as if the rain clouds have gathered and blocked out the sun that radiates through my bedroom window, and my clarity of vision disappears, giving way to a constructed barrage of clouds that creates a barrier to me seeing what's behind them. Don't let the cloud of perfectionism hide God's approval and affirmation radiating over you. Perfectionism wants to break apart and block our image of God as a loving, perfect Father who accepts us we are and receives me as I am! If perfectionism can shatter our image of God as Father and us as His children, we won't rest from a place of position, but we will strive from a place of performance. Before we can get to the place where we take off the mask of perfectionism, we must first acknowledge and accept the fact that God is not a grinder, nor a task master. You don't have to earn God's love, act a certain way, achieve a certain accolade, be acknowledged by a certain person or measure up to receive His approval. There are no preliminary rounds for you to get through to make it into His plans and purposes. If we don't receive this truth and absorb it deep into our hearts, we will use perfectionism as our motivator for self-acceptance. We can work harder, move quicker and jump higher, but it will all lead to disappointment and disillusionment. God is not reviewing, analysing, assessing or judging you, whatever state, stage or season of life you find yourself in; He is accepting of you.

I want to close this chapter with the solution in range and the finish line in sight. Allow yourself to sit with the tension of perfectionism, acknowledge it and then give it to God. Recommit your desire to walk with Him daily. Renew your resolve to work with Him consistently from a place of rest. And refresh your perspective of what 'fruitfulness' and 'achievement' looks like, as you watch Jesus model fruitful living to us through the pages of Scripture and the example He lived. I do not underestimate or want to undermine the struggle so many people feel as they wrestle with this issue of perfectionism. We all process at different paces, and find ourselves in different places, but wherever you are, let your eyes gradually move towards the only perfect person that ever lived, Jesus Christ, and let His perfection cover your weaknesses. When this truth begins to permeate your mind, and shape your life, the skies begin to clear, the sun pierces through the clouds, and as you experience the radiance of God's blessing and His acceptance of you,it will cause you to remove the mask of perfectionism.

Heavenly Father, I choose to take off the mask of perfectionism now. I want to learn to be 'content' in all situations and circumstances and to be at peace, aware that you are in control of all things and the world doesn't rest on my shoulders. I give you my perfectionist tendencies and receive the truth that I can rest in your grace, as a much loved child of God. I take off this mask, and I put on your acceptance, affirmation and acknowledgement of me. Amen.

Chapter Six
– *Insecurity Unmasked*

HE'S THE most successful songwriter in history, his boyhood home has been preserved by the British National Trust, he's one of the world's most famous people, he's been knighted by the Queen (this isn't me before you wonder), he has a personal fortune of hundreds of millions of dollars. Yet, he's insecure. When interviewed by the Sydney Morning Herald in 2002 and asked about his dispute with Yoko Ono over the order in which his and John Lennon's names appeared on songs they wrote, Sir Paul McCartney explained it this way: 'Why does it matter? Because I'm human. And humans are insecure. Show me one who isn't.' We all struggle with the mask of insecurity. We could give a lot of definitions for insecurity, but rather than offering a clinical definition of insecurity, and rather than a Wikipedia type definition of what it is, I want to talk about the feeling it creates and see if you can relate.

I enjoy reading when I get the time, and one book that I stumbled upon was 'Daring Greatly' by Brené Brown. In it, she talks about vulnerability and how the key to experiencing complete wholeness in our lives, is to be vulnerable. The key to experiencing love in your life is being exposed, and she unpacked what does that look like? She says, "most of us are driven by a scarcity mentality when it comes to ourselves." I agree with her diagnosis; the underlying issue that most of us think when we're presented with a challenge or a character flaw in ourselves looks something like this: "I am never _____ enough." You fill in the blank because the sentiment itself is significant, and the specific thing you think you are not qualified for is the very thing that breeds insecurity.

I believe so much of our behaviour that misses the mark of God's calling for our lives is the result of insecurity. Let's look at three things in security does in our lives.

First, insecurity attacks our sanity. We express and experience unnecessary anxiety when we forget that there is a particular purpose God has chosen us to do on the earth. Insecurity makes us worry unnecessarily, and as a result it assassinates our peace and sanity. Second, insecurity sabotages our relationships. We feel like others are going to abandon us or not consistently invest in us, and that insecurity causes other people to overcompensate. So, when we're supposed to be a peace bringer, we become a life taker. Purpose adds value it doesn't take away. Walking in purpose makes us an asset to other people's lives and not a liability. Thirdly, insecurity arrests your success. Insecurity doesn't eliminate your purpose, but it impacts the way you execute it. It's the difference between humility and timidity. Paul had to tell Timothy 1:7, 'God didn't give you the Spirit of fear, but power, love and of a sound mind.' With insecurity having such a detrimental impact in so many areas of our lives, let us explore the root of where it comes from, in our attempt to take off the mask of insecurity.

I have noticed that when I feel insecure, I feel a desperate need to build monuments to myself or for myself, rather than creating an altar to God or building a platform for others. A clear indicator that I'm struggling with the insecurity mask is I begin to crave affirmation. That can be through social media, people following me or liking or commenting on my posts, especially after I have just preached. I feel like maybe I didn't do a good enough job, so to feel good about myself, I fish for security in how others feel I did or didn't do. For you, it could be the need to be noticed in what you wear, how your hair looks, or where you go on vacation. We all have areas of our lives in which we are susceptible to insecurity. The biggest challenge is being honest with ourselves.

It has been said that 'pride is the strength of sin', but I also think pride is a by-product of deep insecurity. Whereas fear causes us to hold back, pride causes us to push ourselves forward, and neither direction pushes us to our destiny; rather, each direction derails us from the plans and purposes God has for our lives. Because ultimately, influence and insecurity are opposites. If we think about the issue of insecurity through a leadership lens for a moment. One of my greatest passions and practices is leadership. I am passionate about watching leaders rise because when leaders rise, those around them rise also but when insecurity plays out in a leader's life, leaders don't hire highly gifted people out of fear of being 'overtaken', and as a consequence they fear becoming 'under appreciated'. They then become a lid on the church, business or organisation's progress. Their insecurity manifests itself by surrounding themselves with people that think like them, act like them, imitate them as well as individuals who prop up their ego, instead of taking things to the next level. I call it the King Saul complex.

King Saul was the first King of Israel, and young David was his greatest asset, but Saul perceived him as his greatest threat. When David defeated Goliath, a group of women started singing songs (some scholars think it could have been a Spice Girl song) about David being a more efficient warrior than Saul, and from that day forward Saul perceived David as a competitor, rather than someone that would complement his kingdom reign and objectives. The principle is simply this: If you are insecure, assets are perceived as threats. This is the 'waterfall' effect. When insecurity starts at the top, it falls down and splashes over the culture as well as the heart and minds of everyone connected to that individual. This is not just the case in leadership; this is the case in our everyday lives.

Insecurity often comes from rejection. Maybe you grew up thinking no one accepts you, appreciates you or acknowledges you. We can turn into chronically reluctant adults who lack confidence and refuse to engage with people different from us. For others, we are insecure because of past traumas: a broken home, your parents divorcing, the unexpected death of a loved one, or in extreme cases, an abuse of power or an abusive relationship, all can open up the door to deep insecurities. With technology inundating us with filtered photos and airbrushed images, we can compare our body image with images of superficial perfection, and it causes us to feel insecure. Whether it's weighing a stone or two more than we would like, hair loss or some form of disability, we can see ourselves in a negative light. The result being withdrawal, depression and self-consciousness that can permeate every interaction and encounter we have with others.

This leads us to what I think is one of the most paralysing dilemmas in the 21st Century. Comparison. We become preoccupied with everyone else, those who seem wealthier, smarter, faster, and so on. This makes us feel overshadowed and robs us of the gifts, opportunities and experiences God has prepared for us. It also robs us of collaborative partnerships that could happen across sectors, industries and spheres of influence. Finally, failure can lead us down the dark path of insecurity. As we invest time and resources into a particular project or endeavour and don't receive a return on our investment, a temporary setback can become a permanent stronghold and stumbling block. It can crush our spirit and cause us to retreat in the future. If this sounds all too familiar to you, you are probably thinking, 'Jon, that's me. What's the solution? How do I shed insecurity in my life?' Glad you asked, here goes.

As I have explored the Bible, and have experienced situations in my own life, I have discovered that to shed the mask of insecurity, we must be in security. It sounds like a simple solution, but it's not simplistic. We tend to embrace the illusion of safety from worldly prestige, possessions and positions as opposed to the absolute assurance of our security in Christ. Secure people are not looking over their shoulders but are strengthening their shoulders so others can stand on them. There have been times in my life when I desperately wanted to hear affirmation or recognition for doing a good job or leading well, and I wanted encouragement, love and reciprocity, and I didn't get it. Often, the people we want it from are the ones closest to us who we feel owe us a pat on the back or words of affirmation, but they just don't come, and that can be deeply painful. But as I grew in my faith, I realised that sometimes God will withhold other people giving me affirmation, even those who maybe should know better, because He wants my affirmation to rest in Him not in what I can do for Him or what people say about my work or best efforts (remember the last chapter?! Perfectionist tendencies!). I had to understand that I don't just have to manage my insecurities, or deal with my insecurities but, or grit my teeth and will myself to overcome or ignore my insecurities, I can actually grow past them! And so can you. How do we do it? We 'cut the but!' (Don't close the book just yet; let me explain…)

How many of us has God called us to do something, given us a dream of an idea for our lives, yet because of our insecurities we come back at Him with 'but'. *But Jon I'm not good enough, but we're in lockdown Jon, but I'm not smart enough, but I didn't go to the right school, but my parents didn't give me the start in life I needed.* We all have a list of buts as long as our arms, but here's what I've learnt: it's really hard to be led by your butt! Try walking with your but out front; you will firstly get some very strange looks, and secondly you will keep butting into things. You see it's hard to move forward when you're living life with your but on display.

I remember the day when God called Chantel and I back to the UK to start SOUL Church; we were living in probably the most amazing city in the world, Cape Town. The UK is cold and dark for 5 months of the year trust me I had some buts! Here's what I realised in that season: if we're ever going to step into our God given future, we're going to have to get over our but! Breakthrough starts with our insecurities where our buts end.

We don't chain our identities to our insecurities. In fact, we chain our identity to what God's Word says, and that breathes a fresh hope, potential and security back into our lives. Every time I think of an obstacle or some form of opposition that can stop me entering into what I am called to conquer as a Christian, I remove the 'but' and I replace it with 'therefore': For example, therefore I am a child of God, therefore no weapon formed against me shall succeed. Therefore God will disprove every tongue that rises against me in judgment. (Isaiah 54:17). In Paul's letter to Timothy, his young mentee, he reminds him that though we can be chained as he was, as a 'physical prisoner', we can also be prisoners to ourselves if God's Word is not chained to our hearts. We need to chain the truth around our hearts. If we tie our identities to God's truth, God's Word can and will lift us above and beyond the insecurities that are holding us back, keeping us down and taking us under.

The Bible states that as children of God, it's part of our inheritance to be secure. We are told that we are joint heirs with Jesus and whatever He has, we get. What confidence that should bring us! We should focus on this truth, and as we focus more and more on the reality of who we are as God's children, we will allow our minds and hearts to be renewed, changed and transformed. We each need to speak what the Bible says about us as children of God to overcome the defeating prison guard insecurity that is in our lives. Christ wants us to break free, and He has given us the keys. The master key of course, is the revelation of how loved we are by God. This truth unlocks every other truth and helps us to walk free and take off the mask of insecurity in our lives.

The New Testament writer John says in one of his letters to the early church community: *'There is no fear in love...but full-grown (complete, perfect) love turns fear out of doors and expels every trace of terror!' (1 John 4:18 AMP).*

Getting a revelation of God's love for you will help you to understand your value isn't in your net worth or your value isn't in your net worth, your relational assets, what you do, what you own or who you know; your worth your worth and values are based on the fact that you are a child of God. This is so important because if we believe God loves us based on what we do or how well we perform, we will never be truly secure and stable in our relationship with Him. I've had to remind myself at times that I am not Soul Church. My identity doesn't come from what I do, or what stage I stand on I am just as important and valuable to Him with a ministry or without. I believe that the very same thing can ring true for you. You are not where you live and, you are not what you do. Whether you're single or married, have children or not, whether you're rich or poor, you are just as important to God as everyone else. We are all equally valuable to God, and He will never love us any more than He loves us right now.

Maxwell Maltz, who wrote 'Psycho Cybernetics', estimates that 95 percent of people in our society have a strong sense of inadequacy. I have no difficulty believing that figure. The only surprise is the other 5 percent. Inferiority, inadequacy and insecurity all go together. Everybody struggles with these feelings. For example, it is rare when celebrities acknowledge and admit anything but the carefully crafted image that's on view to the general public. But this particular excerpt by the singer Madonna reveals that all of us, even celebrities, struggle with insecurities. Sadly, for Madonna, what has made her successful is also what causes pain and suffering in her life: her fear that she will only be 'mediocre,' which to her appears to be a death sentence. She says:

'All of my will has always been to conquer some horrible feeling of inadequacy. I'm always struggling with that fear. I push past one spell of it and discover myself as a special human being and then I get to another stage and think I'm mediocre and uninteresting. And I find a way to get myself out of that. Again, and again. My drive-in life is from this horrible fear of being mediocre. And that's always pushing me, pushing me. Because even though I've become Somebody. I still have to prove that Somebody. My struggle has never ended, and it probably never will.'

Madonna describes and diagnoses 'the cul-de-sac' dilemma that is living from a place of what we do, as opposed to living from a place of security and adequacy in Christ before we have ever achieved or accomplished anything. Madonna's example shows us how a lack of security and sense of inadequacy can have a debilitating impact on one's life. It is as if there is an 'on or off' switch of validation that flicks on or off depending on what external things have been accomplished. From my reading of the Bible, there is no 'on and off' switch when it comes to being a child of God. God's grace is final; the verdict has come in, and you are validated and verified in Him. He won't change His mind about you.

But Jon, you have no clue about my past, my poor choices, what I've done or where I've been. You're right I don't, but God does, yet He still chooses to forgive and keep loving you. Trust God's hold on you, and when you feel yourself loosening your grip on Him, He will never loosen His grip on you. Unlike human love for others, His love is not dependent on you; your candle may flicker, and your passion may wane, but His love for you will never expire. That is why John calls God's love 'perfect love', (1 John 4:17) because it's without flaw, without judgement, and boundless, so we don't have to fear God's love will ever stop or be removed.

God has placed a rope in your hand. It says in the first chapter of the Old Testament book of Judges that God is strong, and He can help you not to fall or stumble. Our Christian walk can often feel like an uphill climb. But Jesus has placed a rope in our hands which is the Word of God. As we unmask insecurity, what we discover is, though it is expressed in a variety of ways, depending on personality, temperament, personal values and learned habits, ultimately, it is another form of fear. If our identity is understanding who we are at our core, it's our essential self. And so, a question I often ask myself on the other side of feeling insecure is this: Who do I believe has the greatest power to determine who I am and what I am worth? If my answer to that isn't God, then I am on dangerous ground, as I am within insecurity's grasp to sweep me up and push me over.

When I feel insecure, and like many of you this is often a daily struggle, I remember God is inviting me to escape the layers of false beliefs, masks and images and find a peaceful refuge in what Jesus says about who I am in Him.

The more we understand our place in Jesus' plan, the more we find it is the end to our feelings of inadequacy and insecurity. Jesus is now your new identity. That is what it means for you if you are a follower of Christ. Underneath all the layers of false self, your true identity can be found as we lay aside the weight of fear that must be removed from our backs. We must remember the first words of the Bible 'In the beginning God.' Not 'in the beginning fame,' not 'in the beginning prestige,' not 'In the beginning more followers or likes.' It didn't start with me, it didn't start with you, or any other created thing, 'in the beginning God....'. We are all in a story that began with God and that must be our reference point for our lives. You and I are in God's story; we have been 'grafted in' firm and secure!

I am often dragged off shopping with Chantel and my two

children, Miracle and Justice, and sometimes that involves going to an indoor shopping centre. What I love about these shopping centres is not only how big they are, but they also provide a map to tell me where everything is. It can be quite overwhelming, especially in busy periods, when everyone is moving at a rapid pace, and I can't find what I'm looking for or where I am meant to be. Therefore, the diagram and directory of the shopping mall is very helpful. When you first look at it though it doesn't make any sense, until you see the sign and words 'you are here.' At once, you know where you are, and you can work your way towards where you need to be. Ultimately, you have to figure out at some point, 'where am I?' And this is a way of thinking that produces an attitude and a spirit of security in our lives. It's opening up God's Word, and realising when you do, 'I am here.' This is my role. I am a child of God. I am called. Chosen. Secure. Handpicked. Meticulously crafted for God. This is my location based on my relationship with Jesus and because of what Christ has done for me. This is my starting point for life, 'I am here.'

Insecurity may fill our world, but it doesn't have to fill our hearts. It will always knock on the door. Just don't invite it in for dinner, and don't offer it a bed for the night. Let's encourage and empower our hearts with the truth of who we are in Christ. I don't know what kind of decision you have to make as we end this chapter. But I write all this to offer a challenge: We must let our identity, not our insecurity, define who we are and lead us as we walk into every situation and circumstance we face and every decision we need to make. If we are going to live from a place of abundance, not lack, and if we are going to be free from the mask of insecurity, we must 'cut the but' and chain the truth. It is then and only then we can stop choking from a lack of truth and enter into all God has for us.

Heavenly Father, I can be in security, instead of living insecure. I can be secure in your love and take hold of my position as a child of God, instead of trying to perform for your acceptance. I take off the mask of insecurity, by stepping into the truth of who I am as a child of God. Loved. Chosen. Called. In Jesus' name! Amen.

Chapter Seven
– *Anxiety Unmasked*

I'M A FOODIE! You put it in front of me, and I will probably eat it. It doesn't matter what type of food it is: Chinese, Indian, Jamaican, Mexican (Chantel's fav)—I'm all in! (Except raw eggs, uncooked tomatoes and guacamole). I try to live as healthily as possible and watch my waistline. But one of my challenges is I have an appetite for a particular delicacy that I can't seem to shake. It fills a big part of my daily diet. It's what I affectionately term: 'The Stress Sandwich'.

'What on earth are you talking about, Jon? What's a stress sandwich?' It is when you put a little slice of today in between the two slices of the regret of yesterday and your anxiety about tomorrow. So, I get two pieces of bread that are represented by all the things that didn't go right yesterday or that I wished were different about yesterday – that is the first slice. The other slice is all the anxiety I have about what might happen, what could happen and what is going to happen, and all the different scenarios playing out in my mind about tomorrow. I take both those pieces together and in between I put today, and that is called a stress sandwich. I would love to say it tastes delicious, that it's nutritious and that it provides sustenance for my life, but it doesn't. In fact, it's the complete opposite. I put on weight that weighs me down so I can't focus. It causes me to carry unnecessary loads that I was never designed to carry. The stress sandwich is the worst sandwich! Sometimes I eat it for breakfast, lunch and dinner. When times are tough, I also have it as a snack in between meals. The problem is, it's filled with dead calories. Despite knowing this, it is what most of us tend to eat for lunch every day. We are chewing on the regrets of our yesterdays and the 'what-if' scenarios of tomorrow.

For many, anxiety isn't just something we consume and fill our stomach with; it is a prevalent fear and emotion hanging over our shoulders. It's a constant sense of dread by our side that is triggered in many area of our lives. For many, it's an invisible enemy that would like nothing more than for you to believe that your life will never be free from its grasp. It's an enemy that traps far too many people and holds its victim hostage in a pit of darkness and defeat. However, here's some good news: you can live free!

The top ten things we worry about in the U.K. (and I'm pretty sure these are universal) are as follows:

10. Pet's health
 9. My dress sense
 8. Whether my partner still loves me
 7. Paying rent/mortgage
 6. Wrinkles
 5. Job security
 4. Debt
 3. My diet
 2. My savings
 1. Getting old

The problem with all these anxieties and with anxious living is it steals our appetite for anything else. That is what it does. Many scientists and doctors have discovered that our stomach's our second brain. Our body is so sophisticated that our stomach talks to our brain. Researchers at UCLA were shocked to find out that ninety percent of the fibre's in one particular nerve carry information to the brain and not the other way around. This means the environment in your gut is a primary system calling the shots with your brain function. The same thing is true when it comes to our spiritual lives. If we are not ingesting the right things, especially if we are not regularly ingesting the Bible, then we are putting ourselves in a situation where the wrong things are talking to us and influencing us the wrong way. We have to make sure we are ingesting the right things, not the anxiety that looks so good for us but is nothing more than dead calories that put on unhealthy weight, but what God is saying.

That is why too much news, too much of Instagram, too much of all that is just too much. We are ingesting more of that stuff than we are ingesting what God says about us. See, the benefit of a healthy relationship with God is we get to rest in God. Jesus said, in 'John 10:10: *The thief comes only to steal and kill and destroy; I have come that they may have life and have it to the full.'* Because of anxious living, what is stolen from us is joy, peace and rest. What is killed in us are hopes, dreams and desires. The abundant life Jesus is describing it not about the absence of issues, but it is a relationship with the One who is taking on those issues and who has overcome them. Even before the entrance of COVID-19, anxiety levels were skyrocketing in our nation. On the face of it, this seems odd as, relatively speaking, we live in an age of unprecedented comfort, convenience and connectivity. So, what's wrong with us?

A powerful story is told of the bombing raids of World War Two where thousands of children were orphaned and left to starve in the UK. After experiencing the fright of abandonment, many of these children were rescued and sent to refugee camps where they received food and shelter. Yet even in the presence of good care, they had experienced so much loss that many of them could not sleep at night. They were terrified they would awake to find themselves once again homeless and hungry. Nothing the adults did seemed to reassure them, until someone thought to send a child to bed with a loaf of bread. Holding onto their bread, the children were able to sleep. If they woke up frightened in the night, the bread seemed to remind them, "I ate today and I will eat again tomorrow."

Hours before he was arrested, Jesus spoke to His disciples about the time ahead of them, days they would face without His physical presence. 'In a little while,' he said, 'you will see me no more, and then after a little while you will see me.' Reasonably, at his words the disciples were confused. 'What does he mean by 'a little while'? We don't understand what he is saying.' They grumbled in anxious fear. Jesus answered with something more than reassurance. He gave them a truth they could hang their hat on. To their confusion and uncertainty, perhaps also to their fears of the worst and visions of the best, Jesus responded: "I have told you these things, so that in me you may have peace. In this world you will have trouble. But take heart! I have overcome the world. John 3:16." It was the last conversation He had with them before going to the cross and dying for the sins of humanity.

Just like those children with bread holding onto what gives them life, Jesus offers us the opportunity to hold on to peace in uncertainty, mercy in the midst of our anxiety and something solid when all is lost. He speaks of peace that can transcend understanding when we cling in gratitude to the one who gives us life. It is worth noting that His use of the word 'peace' here portrays a quiet state of mind, which is infinitely dissimilar to a mind that has been silenced by coercion or despair. But the gospel is good news. It is as if Jesus says, "These things I have spoken to you, so that in me you might be thoroughly quieted by what gives you life."

As I mentioned earlier, in 2008 we moved down to Cape Town, South Africa from the U.K. to be part of a small team to help pioneer Hillsong South Africa. We didn't have much money; we had nowhere to live long term and no salary. But as we boarded BA58 for a night flight over the equator, we felt an overwhelming sense of peace. Why? Because God had given us a promise in His Word, that He would never leave us or forsake us. This spoke of protection, provision and purpose. So even though not everyone understood our decision, and South Africa was commonly known for its many challenges, in the midst of it all, we had peace. You see peace isn't about what is happening around you; it's about what's happening in you. When we hold onto God's promises, we hold onto peace.

When the Apostle Paul wrote down the puzzlingly simple instruction: "Do not worry about anything," he had every reason to be anxious about everything. Thanksgiving could quite easily have been far from him. In prison and facing days fearfully out of his control, even death, Paul was unquestionably holding onto something more solid. *'The Lord is near,'* he wrote from a jail cell. *"Do not be anxious about anything, but in everything, by prayer and petition, with thanksgiving, present your requests to God. And the peace of God, which transcends all understanding, will guard your hearts and your minds in Christ Jesus.' Philippians 4:5-7.* Paul does not promise that followers of Jesus will not see darkness or sorrow any more than he himself was avoiding it, or Jesus himself escaped it. But he does promise, as clearly as Jesus promised the disciples, that there is a solid reason for thanksgiving in the best and worst of times. The Lord who is near in the midst of this darkness has overcome the world in which we will continue to find trouble.

Continuing on this theme of food, somehow even in the midst of trouble Jesus can answer the cries of our hearts with something far more solid than mere wishful reassurance. He told His disciples: *'I am the bread of life. Whoever comes to me will never go hungry, and whoever believes in me will never be thirsty.'* Just like children pacified by the assurance of bread, we are invited to hold the very bread of life, a hope far more solid than anxiety. This is good news for us all, as the statistics surrounding anxiety are nothing short of alarming. Globally an estimated 284 million people experience some form of anxiety on a daily basis. This makes it the most prevalent mental health disorder. Whether men or women, young or old, married or single, dating and waiting – everyone wears the mask of anxiety. It is the most prominent and pervasive human emotion that our generation has to fight. While feeling anxious is not a sin, God doesn't want us to live in a continual state of dread because of life's uncertainties. No one has to live in anxiety; the scripture says it's a choice. Of course, this does not consider the biochemical and medical diagnosis and disorders that many people suffer from. I am not a trained scientist or doctor, so I will be focusing on anxiety from a purely biblical and spiritual perspective. Freedom and peace await those who are willing to give their worries to God and leave them in His hands. Our anxiety belongs to God.

Each day, Jesus sends out an invitation for us to come and sit with Him. But too often we allow our doubts, fears and anxieties to turn our attention away from Him and onto ourselves. *'What will I do? What will they think of me? I feel so....'* As these anxious thoughts multiply, we have a choice: to frantically search for answers in our environment, on our feeds, with our friends and family, and in ourselves; or to do as Jesus taught the disciples, to seek God and His kingdom first (Matthew 6:33). Instead of thoughts that distract us from the One who actually has the answers, we fill our mind with faith-building questions like, What does God want me to do today? What does He want from me? What decisions does He want me to make? The 'what if' anxiety waves that crash over our lives subside in the wake of God's guidance, love and power.

I often think about this on a Sunday morning. As I look around our church, I see such a diverse group of people, and as they sing I think to myself, 'I wonder what it is that they have come into church carrying with them today.' So many worries, anxious thoughts, needs in the room. What always amazes me is when the worship begins, the message goes out and God's presence comes down, it begins to penetrate people's minds and hearts, and anxiety begins to leave the room. Suddenly as God gets bigger, their anxiety gets smaller. The situations in people's lives haven't changed in these few moments in church, but people have changed how they see their situation. Anxiety is out the door!

Here are some practical steps to taking off the mask of anxiety in our lives:

Firstly, stop playing the enemy's games. In my favourite passage in the Bible Paul tells us not to worry about anything. These have to be the four hardest words in the Bible. The enemy wants us to read the verse like this 'Worry about everything'. (Philippians 4:6) That's exactly how so many people live their days. It's a game the enemy loves to play; every morning he wants us to wake up and begin to worry, and not just worry, but worry about everything. I'm continually trying to remove the mask of worry. I'll be totally honest here, I worry about getting old. I dread the prospect of ageing, but it's a part of life and we all have to deal with it. The worst part is when you see a photo of yourself from a few years back and can't believe what's happened! Unless you are my wife who looks younger by the day. I married up.

I worry about this book. I am sitting down now, writing it, thinking 'I wonder if anyone will even read it?' I failed English literature at school, and now I am attempting to write a book.

I worry about my children's future partners: Who will they marry? Where will they live? But worrying does not change anything. Worry will have nothing but a detrimental impact on your life. As you read this verse from Paul, I am sure you are trying to combat it with an 'except". Don't worry about anything "except" my dental appointment this week. Don't worry about anything "except" my phone bill I cannot afford to pay. Don't worry about anything "except" the guy my daughter is dating who is not what I had in mind.

In 2013 when we moved back up to the UK from Cape Town to pioneer SOUL Church, throughout that six-month transition there were countless times I lived daily wearing the mask of anxiety. 'Don't worry about anything... except where will we live?' I just always add an exception to the verse. The enemy's plan for our lives is we keep adding the word except to our situations so we have license to worry.

Secondly, give your concerns to God. Instead of being anxious, pray about everything and give your concerns to God. Paul says, 'I'm going to give you an alternative to the enemy's games, I'll take it from here. God can handle our worries!' Often the first place we run to with our worries are the people least likely to be able to help us. Some of the people you are sharing your worries with are draining your faith. You need to protect yourself. Paul realised the enemy was playing games, and he wasn't going to listen to the enemies lies.

Thirdly, don't let your anxieties get the best of you. When a wasp lands on you, you don't say, "I'll take care of it in a minute." No, you splat it before it can bite you (apologies wasp lovers, personally I'm just not a fan). Be equally decisive with your anxieties. The moment they land, deal with them. Before you rush to diagnose that mole as a cancer, have it examined; instead of assuming you'll never get out of debt, consult a financial expert. Be a doer, not an overthinker. Over thinking everything so often causes anxiety in our lives. Anxiety is a word of unbelief or unreasoning dread. We have no right to allow it. Full faith in God puts it to rest. The crosses we bear over anxiety concerning the future aren't crosses that come from God, so give your anxiety to God and leave it with Him!

Fourthly, you can list your anxieties. For one week, make a list of the things you worry about most. Children? Health? Money? Marriage? Job? Your football team? These aren't one-time worries that come and go quickly. They're things that make you constantly and consistently uneasy, so begin to review them. Ask yourself how many of them have actually turned into reality? Charles Spurgeon said, 'Our worst misfortunes never happen... most of our miseries lie in anticipation.'

Next, analyse them. You'll detect recurring themes in your life that may become obsessions: what people think of you; the fact that heart disease, cancer and Alzheimer's run in your family; the fear that you won't have enough to live on when you get old. Identify each fear and pray specifically about it. And remember no anxious thought is either too big or too small for God not to get involved.

Finally, live in today. God has promised to meet your needs daily, not weekly or annually. He'll give you what you need when you need it! The writer to the Hebrews reassured us that we can *'therefore come boldly to the throne of grace, that we may obtain mercy and find grace to help in time of need'* (Hebrews 4:16). There are 807,361 words in the Bible (trust me, count them, and let me know what you conclude), but you'll search in vain for a single mention of the specific word "worry." This is not a word Jesus uses. It's not in God's vocabulary, and it shouldn't be in yours either.

In my own personal walk and battle with anxiety, I have found asking others to help is a great tool to taking off the mask. As unique as God has made you, other people are facing the same fears, too. By "telling" on your anxieties, they begin to lose their power. Remember: *'Two are better than one...If one falls down, his friend can help him up. But pity the man who falls and has no one to help him up!'* (Ecclesiastes 4:9-10). Share your feelings with someone you trust and ask them to pray with you. I have a group of four friends and spiritual fathers I open up to when needed. I get their opinion, ideas and wisdom on the specific situation.

One of the questions I am famously known for is 'what would you do if you were in my position?' You see, because they're not wearing mask of anxiety like I am, they are able to think a lot more logically and give me a much more measured response. I wonder who you have in your world, that your trust, that you could ask for help?

People are more willing to help than you might imagine. Less anxiety on your part often means more happiness on those closest to you.

I also find focusing on God and not myself enables me to get the correct perspective on the situation I am anxious about. Jesus concludes a call to an anxiety-free existence, with this challenge: '*Your heavenly Father already knows all your needs. Seek the Kingdom of God above all else, and live righteously, and he will give you everything you need*' (Matthew 6:8). A wise preacher once said: 'If you seek wealth, you'll worry about every pound. If you seek health, you'll fear every blemish and bump. If you seek popularity, you'll obsess over every conflict. If you seek safety, you'll jump at every crack of the twig. But if you focus each day on God's kingdom, 'He will give you everything you need.' An unknown poet wrote: "Said the robin said to the sparrow, 'I should really like to know, why these anxious human beings rush around and worry so.' Said the sparrow to the robin, 'Friend, I think that it must be, that they have no heavenly Father such as cares for you and me.'"

A story is told of a missionary group in Paraguay who discovered a tribe of natives that lived in a remote part of the jungle next to a large spacious river. The native tribe was utterly convinced that the large river was filled with demons and evil spirits, and as a consequence they were too scared to cross it. Disease and death were rampant among their population, and the death count was rising on a daily basis. They desperately needed help, medicine and care or the whole native tribe would be obliterated and extinct forever. The only possible way to get the tribe some help was to traverse that river they were scared to cross. The visiting missionary explained to the native tribe that the river was not full of evil or demons, but it was fine to cross. However, the tribe was too scared and didn't listen. So, the missionary reached down into the river and with his hand splashed himself with the water, and he said to them once more, "Look, it is not evil. It has no power. You do not have to be full of anxiety and fear at the thought of crossing this river." But again, it was to no avail. So he decided to wade deep into the river and splash around. He looked back at them and signalled to them to join him in the water. But his words were ignored and fell upon deaf ears.

The missionary was so consumed with concern to see this tribe made well and healed that in one final moment of desperation he plunged into the large river. He swam beneath the surface until he reached the other side, and when he struggled up, pushing himself onto the shore, he threw a victorious fist into the air. He turned and faced the natives standing on the other side of the river. When he did that, there was a huge round of applause and a shout that rose up as an echo around the basin of the river and one after another the native tribe clambered into the water and rigorously swam across the river they had previously been so anxious about crossing. The missionary had to become an example to the tribesmen of overcoming the anxiety of crossing that river in order to set the tribe free from the anxiety and fear. To put it another way, to help them take off their mask, he took his off as he swam across the river. In the same way, Jesus Christ swam across the river through His death and resurrection. He swam the river of anxiety and was tempted like us yet without sin. He swam across the river of financial concerns and relational splits and victoriously swam out on the other side. We have nothing to be anxious about because Jesus has already made a pathway of provision for us to safely cross over to the other side.

If there's something lingering over your life, threatening your peace, your walk with God, your home, your marriage, your family or your finances, take it to the Lord. He is your example. Don't let anxiety rule. Get up, get perspective, worship God and watch Him work in your life. There is a lot of confusion between fear and anxiety. I like this definition that distinguishes and differentiates the two: Anxiety and fear are cousins but not twins. Fear sees a threat. Anxiety imagines one. What is your imagination focused on daily? Whatever occupies your thoughts regularly, ultimately occupies you. King David, an Old Testament Bible character said when he was afraid, he put his trust in God (Psalm 56:3). Another translation says, when he was filled with anxiety, he focused his attention on God. Notice, David did not say: 'I never struggle with anxiety'. Anxiety will always attack, and when it strikes, a battle begins. But we have been promised that if we stand in what we know, we will win the war. This is important to note This is important to note, that even as believers, we have been told that we will have anxieties. But we can fight back when anxiety attacks.

For example, 1 Peter 5:7 says, 'Cast all your anxieties on him, because he cares for you.' It does not say, you will never feel any anxieties. It says, when you have them, cast them on God. When the mud splatters your windshield and you temporarily lose sight of the road and start to swerve in anxiety, turn on your wipers and squirt your windshield washer. The windshield wipers are the promises of God that clear away the mud of unbelief, and the windshield washer fluid is the help of the Holy Spirit. The battle to be freed from anxiety is a dependence on the Holy Spirit's direction, empowerment and enablement. The work of the Spirit and the Word of truth. These are the great faith-builders. Without the softening work of the Holy Spirit, the wipers of the Word just scrape over the blinding clumps of anxiety and unbelief on the windshield. Both are necessary: the Spirit and the Word. We read the promises of God and we pray for the help of His Spirit. And as the windshield clears so that we can see the welfare that God plans for us (Jeremiah 29:11), our faith grows stronger and the swerving of anxiety straightens out and knocks anxiety to the curb.

As we draw this chapter to a close, can I encourage you every time you have a concern or an anxious thought, write it down and drop it into a container in the kitchen or the office, which says: 'This belongs to God'. These four words can dramatically change your day, as you give God every single one of your anxious thoughts, however big or small. Show God you're serious about living life free from the mask of anxiety. Take it to Him, talk it through with Him, leave it with Him. God created you to be a warrior not a worrier, now walk in your God given freedom.

Heavenly Father, I have been an anxious worrier for long enough. This mask has been weighing me down and hindering me from seeing things clearly. Give me your perspective, and as I take off this mask, I ask for you to give me fresh vision, so I too, like the apostle Paul, can say that the eyes of my heart will be enlightened. In Jesus' mighty name I pray! Amen.

Chapter Eight
– *Inferiority Unmasked*

It has been said that inferiority within a person is like fireworks with a lit fuse; it's only a matter of time until they explode, and when they do, they hurt everyone within close proximity! One example of this happening and where we see the drawbacks of inferiority in a person, is through the life of a brilliant, yet flawed, American leader, Alexander Hamilton (Have you seen the musical?). Hamilton had an incredible mind, and he was a gifted, persuasive speaker. However, the unfortunate thing was, Hamilton was also deeply insecure and felt a deep sense of inferiority in his life. He obsessed over his personal image and what he looked like; he launched vicious verbal assaults on anyone who criticised or challenged him. And tragically, his sense of inferiority literally killed him. He couldn't take off the mask which blinded him from seeing who he was, and that caused him to fall short over who he could be!

Hamilton's life illustrates the qualities of a person who is wearing the mask of inferiority in his or her life. Hamilton wearing the mask of inferiority caused him to push people away. Hamilton's intelligence and leadership ability caught the eye of George Washington, who handpicked him as his personal aide. In this role, he drafted important reports on the general's behalf. However, when Washington challenged him, Hamilton took offence. Hamilton refused to accept the olive branch extended by Washington after this incident and Hamilton alienated himself from the most respected man in the United States.

People that wear the mask of inferiority may at first sight seem paranoid and insecure, but oftentimes, their inferiority complex is the result of some unhealed hurt. For instance, Alexander Hamilton's inferiority complex can be traced all the way back to the trauma experienced during his formative years. In the space of five years, Hamilton's father abandoned him, his mother died, his guardian committed suicide, and his aunt, uncle and grandmother passed away. It's hard to imagine how much all of these tragedies must have impacted him and had a permanent hold on his identity.

A sense of inferiority can be really difficult to recognise in ourselves, psychologists call it our 'blind spot', and it's impossible to remedy on our own. Everyone has a degree of it. The most urgent need for a person wrestling with inferiority is to seek help from a trusted friend, or even a professional advisor. Through conversation with a trustworthy confidant, we can identify areas of inferiority, uncover their roots and begin the process of taking off its mask once and for all.

Over the years, I have noticed a frequent pattern in people that I have known or pastored not so dissimilar to Alexander Hamilton. Whether young or old, male or female, rich or poor, we are all secretly fighting feelings of inferiority. We secretly wonder whether we really measure up to others, to God and to our own standards and expectations for our lives. We fear deep down that we don't have what it takes in any given moment or particular situation. Maybe it's in your inner world, your character, where there is a crack that you try hard to hide. It could be something you watch on a screen that has the gravitational pull to drag you back into old habits and ways of thinking. Many people spend their lives fighting these tensions.

In a previous chapter, I talked about the sense of inadequacy I felt before speaking to thousands of people at Hillsong Conference at the O2 arena. But if I'm honest, I feel that sense of inadequacy on a weekly, sometimes daily basis. I wish the whispers of doubt could be muted, or the regular rattle of my inner critic could be ignored. Before I lead a service or speak on a Sunday, when I have to enter into a difficult conversation, situation or conflict, I am constantly praying this simple, yet effective prayer, 'Lord, help'. I remind myself that I am God's workmanship, created for good works 'in advance' (Ephesians 2:10). Where do you need to remember you are God's workmanship? The reason it is so important for us to remember this is because if we feel inferior our default operating system will be 'scarcity' not 'abundance'. Chantel and I have an evening routine with our two children; first of all, we play football in the living room, which always ends in tears (as someone has to lose), then we tuck our two little tinkers into bed and declare God's truth over their young lives and remind them that they have an abundant life in Christ.

This is our prayer:

Father God, As Miracle & Justice go to sleep tonight, they will know they are the righteousness of God in Christ JESUS. We thank you that they are the head and not the tail. Above and not beneath. The lenders and not the borrowers. They will always have friends because they are friendly, be quick learners, wise decision makers and positive contributors to their world. May they sleep in peace tonight, in JESUS' name. Amen.

Apart from the spiritual benefits, it helps them develop and wire their brain to live from a place of blessing and generosity, as opposed to having a worldview that they must react to everything in the world and feel helpless. It also helps them recognise who they are now in their present so they can take the next step in their journey of becoming who God created them to be. I truly believe encouragement is like oxygen to the soul. Every heart needs it, not just at some point in their life, but at some point during each day.

Every person needs to hear a "wonderful" or "that was great". Or "you are really good at that." Of course, it is not a substitute for the affirmation of God, but it's a much-needed supplement because there is a battle going on for the notification bell of our hearts. No one has ever died from an overdose of encouragement!

Companies spend billions of dollars to convince us that we are inferior and that there is a gap between where we are and where we need to be. Not smart enough. Not good looking enough. Not resourced well enough. It causes inadequacy to indwell in our hearts. This sense of inferiority can go right back to our earliest memories and moments as children. I know people who experience feelings of inferiority because they grew up always struggling financially. They never lived in the 'right' places and never wore the 'right' clothes. Even in school, they felt that they did not measure up academically, socially or relationally to the other kids. Their sense of failure and embarrassment at not looking good or feeling right transferred to their own state of being mentally, physically and spiritually during every season of life.

Inferiority is miserable. And the misery of inferiority is never what God intended for us. The seed of inferiority usually takes root in the impressionable hearts of the young and thrives in an atmosphere of competition and comparison. This kind of baggage can have debilitating and enslaving repercussions and ramifications in almost every area of life. I know that feelings of inadequacy can cause avoidance of healthy challenges or stepping out of comfort zones, or taking risks. People's low self-esteem cripples confidence, and comparison steals contentment. We have never been more in danger of comparing our lives to other people in the midst of our technological and social media revolution. As a pastor, I think social media is an amazing connector, and the social media sphere is an incredibly vast digital mission field to utilise and engage with. What I think is critical, however, is that we manage it properly so that the exposure to what other people are doing doesn't awaken an appetite in us for someone else's path or purpose. In other words, we live with destination disease; we always want to be somewhere or have something else. It's also been described as FOMO—Fear Of Missing Out.

How many times have I woken up ready to take on a new day, picked up my phone, scrolled through Instagram, and within minutes felt inadequate as I look through the lens of someone else's world?

I have found that the quickest way to feel inferior is to compare what God is doing in me, in the season I am in, with what is happening with someone else. That causes us to feel intimidated and inferior. If you're playing the comparison game, the better others do, the worse you look, and the worse they do, the better you look. I have heard it said that most of us wait until no one is watching to do something wrong, and we wait until someone is watching to do something right. That's not human nature. We must remember: success and fruitfulness are two very different things. Jesus' success on the cross was seen as a defeat and foolishness by the world's standards and comprehension, yet it was the very power for salvation. To be fruitful means to be faithful. Faithful to your assignment and faithful to living out the good works God has created you to walk in.

I believe three things can help us as we begin the process of taking off the mask of inferiority in our lives. Are you ready? Here we go!

DISCIPLINE

I find a good way to stop feeding the beast that is inferiority, and a good first step to start untying its mask, is to limit my screen time. Have a day where you turn off your phone. Go scriptural before you go digital. Spend time in God's Word. His Word won't open up to you if you keep it closed. Many of us feel a sense of inferiority when it comes to reading God's Word. We can feel overwhelmed and intimidated by the size of the book. However, a good rule of thumb to remember is: The goal is not to get through the Bible—the goal is to get the Bible through you. I recently heard Pastor Rick Warren of Saddleback Church encourage a group of young leaders to keep their Bibles open besides their beds and keep their phones switched off in the kitchen at night; it's a good rule to live by. The Bible is an open invitation not a closed book. Maybe you struggle with sleep or anxiety at night; having the Bible open beside your head is a constant reminder God is with you.

When we make a regular routine and rhythm in God's Word, suddenly His voice becomes our standard and not other people's context. You're never going to fully give yourself to what you need to do until you stop comparing yourself to other people and what they can do. Remaining in the constant cycle of comparison will cause us to sit in our feelings of inadequacy, as opposed to standing in who we are and embracing our God-given identity.

DISCOVERY

I believe the reason the apostle Paul could say with confidence that he wasn't inadequate was because he discovered, then stood in the love of God and reminded himself of it regularly. Paul told his churches that true significance comes from knowing and understanding the full dimensions of God's love. This knowledge is our anchor when our emotions and feelings of worthlessness overwhelm us or thoughts of failures from the past overwhelm us. Notice that the Lord doesn't say He'll give us all the qualities and possessions we think will overcome our sense of inferiority. Instead, He promises to strengthen us 'in the inner person' (Ephesians 3:16).

CONFIDENCE

We need confidence in God releasing us from our sense of inadequacy. "I can't" are words that we often use to dismiss our responsibility to do something God wants us to do. As frightening as those kinds of emotions and feelings are, we must never mistake them for reasons to avoid the direction God has for us in life. Let's look at a young character in the Old Testament, a teenager by the name of Jeremiah. God had prepared him to be "a prophet to the nations" (Jeremiah 1:5). Yet when God revealed His plans to Jeremiah, Jeremiah didn't understand that God was giving directives instead of inviting a discussion. Jeremiah immediately objected, 'I cannot speak, for I am a youth' (verse 6). It is not clear how old Jeremiah was, but it didn't matter to God. He didn't accept his objections. Instead, the Lord provided what Jeremiah would need to succeed: His enablement (verse 7), His presence (verse 8) and the words to speak (verse 9).

We can all connect and relate to Jeremiah's objections. I remember the first time I put on the mask of inferiority, I told myself, "I'm not that smart; I'm not that intelligent." Yet we must pay attention to the encouragement Jeremiah no doubt drew from God's words, and consequently we can, too. God not only promises, but He also equips everyone He appoints to serve Him. Jeremiah told how "the Lord reached out His hand and touched my mouth and said to me, 'Now, I have put my words in your mouth'" (verse 9). God enables us to perform the task He is sending us to do.

July 13th 2014 was a huge milestone day in our lives as we launched SOUL Church UK. At last, the dream we had carried for years had become a reality. What people didn't realise that day was, as the service was beginning at 10am, I was hiding in the bathroom crouched on the floor feeling overwhelmed and inferior; the mask was real. Thoughts of why me? I am too young, unqualified; so many triggers were going off in my head. The reality is we have all experience a July 13th moment somewhere and at some point in our lives.

I am still learning how to overcome and take off the mask of inferiority; it is certainly not easy, and if I'm honest, it is a constant daily battle but a battle I'm committed to keep fighting.

When it comes to my own weaknesses and sense of inferiority, I tend to shift between two different extremes, both of which stem from wearing the mask of inferiority. I either wallow deeply in my weaknesses, wishing God would take them away, or I try to hide them and pretend they don't exist. When we ask God to take them away, we must remember the apostle Paul did the same thing. He had what the Bible calls 'a thorn in the flesh', and he asked God to take it away from him three times, only for God to say that His grace was sufficient enough for Paul, and His power is made perfect in weakness. We must acknowledge and admit we have a weakness, it becomes the seed by which humility grows in the soil of our hearts. Humility, not self-denial, enables us to pick up and carry Christ's strength when our inadequacy is embraced, not ignored or denied.

I read a story about a famous person who wanted to learn tennis as a hobby. Naturally, this person was nervous about their first lesson, and the first thing the tennis instructor said to this person didn't help calm the nerves: "All right, let me see exactly what I'm working with here." The immediate response was defensive, "I have no idea what I am doing." What the instructor said next confused the famous person. "Perfect. That is just the way I like it. You are the perfect person to work with." He went onto explain how people come all the time knowing just enough about tennis to make them impossible to teach and coach. They don't want to trust a new method or way of playing because they are used to the way they have always played. They then try to show the coach how much they know instead of learning what he has to teach them.

In a similar vein, I wonder if God speaks back to our weakness like the tennis instructor spoke to the famous person "You are by far my favourite type of person to work with." When we pray and say, "God, I have no idea what I am doing when I stand up to lead hundreds of people every week, so why am I here?" Humility unlocks the bridge to Christ crossing over and lending us His strength. Pride, on the other hand, is the greatest barrier to receiving grace for our inferiority and inadequacy. Weakness can work for us if we put our weakness in the hands of a mighty God.

I'm personally inviting you to join me in to the fight against unmasking inferiority using these following four steps.

The first step is to develop 'a sense of of belonging'. We need to recognise that we belong to God the Father. Those who belong to God receive God's care, provision and protection as His children. That is where our confidence is found.

The second step is to develop 'a sense of pride'. A sense of pride is closely related with value. Our sense of pride changes according to how much we value ourselves. When we purchase something, we determine the value of the merchandise depending on its cost. When we evaluate a house, we also determine its value according to cost. After encountering Jesus, we realise that He paid the price for our salvation with His own life. Because of God's love for us, He gave away His one and only Son, Jesus. In that sense, our worth is Jesus. We are as valuable as the sacrifice of Jesus. Most of all, we are not a commodity. We are the masterpiece of God. A commodity can be compared, and when compared with a better product, its value can be diminished. However, a masterpiece cannot be an object of comparison. Because of its uniqueness and rarity, it has an eternal value. I am a priceless masterpiece! Stick that on the fridge! Or put it on your mirror in the morning! Remember this precious truth about yourself.

The third step is to develop 'a sense of confidence'. A sense of confidence is related to our ability. The Apostle Paul confessed, *'I can do all this through him who gives me strength'* (Phil. 4:13). God pours out His power on us through the Holy Spirit. The Holy Spirit is the Spirit of wisdom, strength and understanding. I have learned the way to allow Jesus to capture all my thoughts. All things begin with our thoughts. An inferiority complex begins with a sense of inferiority. No one can make us feel inferior if we don't consider ourselves to be inferior. Just as the Apostle Paul chose to believe, if we could believe that we can do all things through Him who gives us strength, then we will be able to do all things. Right living begins with right believing!

The fourth step is to advance with 'a sense of purpose'. We were not born into this world by chance. We were born with purpose. We were born to win! In fact, even before you were born, millions of your siblings were in a battle called the egg, and sperm (not spoon) race. It only takes one sperm to fertilise a female's egg but there's 200 million sperm competing. You took some hits, you might have tripped along the way, you nearly got pipped at the finish line—but you made it; there was only one winner that day! YOU!

Every time you feel inferior, like you're an accident or you don't have a purpose in this life, remind yourself that you were born a winner! You remain a winner! Life has a way of stealing that gold medal from around our necks and replacing it with a mask. We weren't just born to win, either; we were born with a sense of purpose. God has sent us to this world to accomplish something. We were born into this world entrusted with God-given tasks. In order to complete the tasks, God has given each of us talents and gifts. Through our talents and gifts, we have been called to bless others and become a channel of God's blessings. We are happy and feel worthwhile when we serve others according to our talents and gifts. No child of God is inferior. We are all valuable beings. You are valuable in God's eyes. The truth is, there are always people more talented and more qualified. Someone does know their Bible better. Someone does spend more time in prayer. Some are more humble, selfless and equipped to lead. But when God calls who He wills, and asks us to speak, serve and lead, we are invited to embrace the call and obey. I love this quote by Steven Furtick 'God qualifies the unqualified', I feel like this has been the mantra over my life over the past few years. God makes up the bits where I fall short or don't have the right qualifications or experience. I stand tall on Christ's shoulders. On His shoulders, God gives us the position, the perspective to proclaim this truth we have already identified:

'You are a chosen, a royal priesthood, a holy nation,
a people for his own possession, that you may proclaim
the excellencies of him who called you out of darkness
into his marvelous light'. (1 Peter 2:9).

Ultimately, we must embrace to replace. Embrace the role we have been given and reject the inferiority that comes with wanting someone else's life, underestimating, and undervaluing our own. So, let's embrace who we are. Let's embrace our weaknesses. It does not sell God short of His abilities, desires and intentions to change and transform our lives. We are not imprisoned in our present state or condition.

In Acts 2:1 we read, *'They day of Pentecost came, and they were all there of one accord'* This phrase "One accord" comes from a musical term which means multiple notes playing a harmonious melody (FYI I used to play the trumpet and it wasn't harmonious for my neighbours—it was erroneous!). You may not be as gifted as some in a certain area, but it doesn't mean your gift doesn't have value. Don't compare your gift to someone else's gift as you are not called to play the same note as another; you are called to play your note. There are no big gifts and little gifts; yes, there may be gifts more visual and prominent to people, but no gift is more important than another when it comes to God's economy. Every instrument in the orchestra has significance and importance; what is imperative is that every musician keeps his or her eyes on the conductor.

When you and I are tempted to wear the mask of inferiority, remember: God not only uses the weak, but His power is made perfect in weakness (2 Corinthians 12:9-10). Christians should not be like the world and hide their weakness in the basement of their lives. Instead, like Paul, we boast in our weaknesses, for, when we are weak, then we are strong. He alone strengthens timid hearts, emboldens scared disciples and makes the weak strong as we lift our eyes from our frailty to Him. So, with that in mind, we might feel small, but as long as He is big in our eyes, we can take off the mask of inferiority. In Jesus, there is no inferiority. No matter how unqualified you may feel, you can be a tool used by God. The greatest ability is availability. Whenever you wrestle with your own sense of self or what God has called you to do, though you seem small in your own eyes, although you seem small in your own eyes, remember that God goes with you like He went with Jeremiah.

Heavenly Father, today I take off the mask of inferiority. I thank you that you made me more than enough when you died and rose again for me. I stand firm in my position as a much-loved child of God and walk in the confidence of knowing that in every opportunity, and when I face every obstacle, I am more than enough with you by my side. Amen.

Chapter Nine
– *Disappointment Unmasked*

SOME DAYS you wake up and could never expect what would occur that would change your life forever. February 2nd, 2018 was one of those days for Chantel and I. As our two children were climbing into the car for what was meant to be a normal school morning routine—Jackets on? Teeth brushed? Hair straight? Let's go!, just before we closed the front door the phone rang. It was Chantel's Auntie in California. Something wasn't right. There was a long silence, then the news: Chantel's dad had just been a victim in a drive-by shooting in downtown Los Angeles, and it didn't look like he would make it. Suddenly Chantel's world fell apart in those few short seconds. Two hours later the worst news possible followed, Joe Cruz, her dad, who had only just come back into her life just two years earlier, had died. Disappointment, devastation and grief beyond belief. Over the next few hours and days, I watched as Chantel grappled with coming to terms with what had just taken place. Overcome with so many emotions and feelings, somehow Chantel managed to keep going, live to face another day and come to terms with a life-changing disappointment.

Like Chantel, maybe you have experienced immense disappointment in your life. When this happens, it feels as if the firm foundation we stand on in the good times gets rocked and can feel as though it's cracking beneath us in the difficult times. Chantel had good days and bad days in the weeks and months following on from the tragedy, but one thing remained the same in the midst of her pain and disappointment, she knew God was still faithful. She didn't dismiss the reality of her shock and pain; she entered into the process of grieving for her father and went through a process of healing and rebuilding. However, what helped Chantel get through this season of her life was that she resisted the temptation to put on the mask of fear, as appealing and attractive as it looked, and instead let her tears flow, her frustration show, and wrestled with the difficult questions such loss can bring.

When I think about disappointment in my life, I think about how I often irrationally react instead of responding to it. Instead of charging forward with courage and confidence, I stay in the stalls, projecting my past experiences onto my present expectations. I feel this is so subtle, but so significant. I love the story about Édouard Calaparède, he was a Swiss psychologist. In 1911, he was treating a patient with no short-term memory. This patient was in his late forties. At the start of every appointment Édouard and his patient would customarily shake hands. One day, Édouard decided to perform a small experiment. When his patient reached out his hand to shake his, he had a pin concealed in his hand, and he pricked him with it. The patient quickly withdrew his hand in pain; a few minutes later, he had no memory of this pinprick. But from that moment on, he would not shake hands with Edouard. He wasn't sure why, but he felt like he couldn't completely trust him. The residue of pain kept him from reaching his hand out.

I like to think of disappointment a bit like a pinprick. It really hurts, and when I experience a disappointment, especially of the faith variety when I've stepped out, trusted and believed, I stop reaching out my hand towards God. We pull back. We can't always identify why we don't completely trust in God, but our disappointment keeps us from reaching out and stepping out in faith again. Our faith moves from trusting God to just knowing Him.

I've discovered that if I'm going to experience progress in any area of my life, I have to confront the layers of dormant disappointments in my past. Disappointments can wreak havoc in our lives, if we don't face them, acknowledge the hurt and work through them. All of us have experienced disappointments in our lives, some far greater than others.

One of my biggest disappointments was when I was seventeen years old. Anyone who knows me well, knows that I am an avid

Norwich City fan. Today, I have the privilege of being Norwich City's Club chaplain, and so you can imagine how I felt, when at seventeen I had a trial at Norwich City in the position of goalkeeper. I was on trial with Robert Green who went onto play for England, and I went onto play for my church (We made it hey!). At the end of the trial, the goalkeeping coach, Martin Thomas, was brutal to me and said to me 'you just aren't good enough'. I remember the pain and disappointment I felt; it was as if the pin-prick didn't just go into my hand, but right into my heart. Hearing those words stung, and it felt like my life was finished and my career was over; and the disappointment really cut me deep. When all your dreams are dashed in those few words, it's devastating. One statement had set me off on a trajectory of withdrawal and confusion. However, I remembered what Jesus had told His disciples, that in this world, we will have trouble (John 16:33). We will face disappointments. We will mess up, make mistakes, fail, have regrets, but in the midst of these things, we must remember that Jesus has overcome the world. That is how we overcome what comes over us.

Jesus told His disciples three times to 'be of good cheer.' In other words: Cheer up lads! How can we be of good cheer in the midst of disappointment? I believe it is because we don't project our circumstances onto the character of God; instead, we view our circumstances through the lens of God's character. The way I got through my disappointment as a seventeen-year-old teenager, when my dreams had been dashed and my favourite football team rejected me, was to trust that God had a bigger plan for my life. Whenever you experience disappointment you have to lean back on trust, trust that God has a plan. I now look back on that disappointment, and realise God had different ideas for my future. If I had become a footballer, I would never be leading a church, I would never have met my wife Chantel (the luckiest girl on the planet) in Sydney Australia at Bible college, and I wouldn't have my two beautiful children! And you probably wouldn't have this book in your hand (maybe you wish I'd been a footballer :-)

One of my favourite Bible verses is Romans 8:28: *'And we know that in all things God works for the good of those who love him, who have been called according to his purpose.'* I cling onto that verse and look back on my past and say thank you for letting me go through the trenches of disappointment, and the valleys, so I can now experience the blessing and favour of God. Therefore, there is purpose in our disappointment. If we decide not to swim in the swamp of misery but instead embrace the mystery, God will do a miracle on the other side of our hurt. It is true for me, and it will be true for you.

I don't know what pain you are experiencing in your life. Perhaps it is a divorce, a wayward child, the death of a loved one during the pandemic, a failed business, a broken relationship. Whatever it is, I am confident that God will take your fractured pieces and use them for His bigger purpose. God is painting your life on a canvas far bigger than we could ever comprehend. The dimensions of His canvas are eternal, the brush He's painting with is limitless, and if we allow Him to take our broken, fractured and fragmented pieces and use them for His purposes, our lives can be changed, transformed and rebuilt for His good, and ultimately ours as well.

As I've mentioned throughout this book: I love reading the Bible. I believe every book of the Bible can tell us something significant, and I also love the section that's been described as 'the minor prophets'. The minor prophets have major truths to tell us. One of those prophets is a guy named Haggai. He wrote a book in 520 BC. The Babylonians had invaded Israel, kidnapped their people and taken them back to Babylon (modern day Iraq) and destroyed Solomon's temple in Jerusalem. Approximately fifty years later, some of the refugees returned to Jerusalem and their first task was to rebuild their city, their infrastructure and systems, but most importantly their temple. The people were frustrated, overwhelmed, and disappointed at what had taken place. They felt as though the task was impossible, and God sent the prophet Haggai to cheer them up. We can all relate to the people Haggai was speaking to. There are certain moments in life when seasons just seem to be laced with one disappointment after the other. And as a result, many people who used to follow Jesus no longer do simply because disappointment has derailed their faith. Sometimes we get so tied to the past that we can't see any hope for our future.

So how do we begin the process of taking off the mask of disappointment in our lives? I believe we have a choice when it comes to disappointment. It can make you bitter. Or it can make you better. The choice is ours. We have a choice to make every time we face a new disappointment: Will I use this? Or will I waste it? Will I get something out of this? Or will I let this get the best of me? As a leader that deals in relationships, I face disappointment on a regular basis. A practice that helps me process my disappointment, that I believe is both practical and spiritual is outlined below.

When I experience disappointment I turn to a clean sheet of paper in my notebook. I take a deep breath and break down the elements of my disappointment into four different and distinct categories. I put my disappointments and my frustration in an organised format to help me get it out of my system, and to help me make sure I'm processing the pain head on. I remember that God is not overwhelmed or intimidated by my disappointments, nor is He scared of my honest feelings. He knows them all anyway, and so this exercise allows me to be honest with God, but it also enables me to manage my emotions so my emotions don't manage me. I promise you, if you implement these steps into your life, you will be able to handle disappointment in a healthy way.

STEP ONE: REFLECTION

Dealing with disappointment in a systematic way begins with unfiltered reflection. You've got to stare down your disappointment before you can deal with it in a productive way. Ideally, this process would begin with prayer. And your prayer would be filled with gratitude, along with acceptance of God's perfect and holy will for your life. In reality, most of us need a lot of help getting to that point. I generally start my process of reflection by talking it out with a few people I trust. I have to be selective about who I'm reflective with, because when the wound of disappointment is fresh, I may say some things that I'll want removed from the record in time. But it's very important that I can tell a few close people how I really feel in a pretty raw way. They can affirm the stuff that's valid and talk me down off the ledge about the stuff that's not.

You may be more introspective. Your process may begin with you and a legal pad, emptying your disappointments like buckets so you can have the capacity to bring them to others when the time is right. Above all, don't neglect to take it to the Lord in prayer. When you do, respectfully state your disappointment to Him. He already knows about it much more comprehensively than you do. And He can handle it. Besides, He's the one in the best position to do something about it. Face your disappointment. What's never confronted in your life will never change. Don't try to sneak up on it from behind. Half the time when you stand toe to toe with your disappointments, you'll discover that they're not nearly as big as you made them out to be. The other half of the time, at least now you know what you're up against.

STEP TWO: ASK QUESTIONS

You've admitted your disappointment. You've laid out your frustrations before God, inviting the supernatural involvement of His Spirit. Now you've got to follow up your reflections with questions. Personally, I start listing every question associated with my disappointment that comes to my mind, indiscriminately, as quickly as I can scribble them down. It's rapid, and it's random. But I can't get the right answers until I identify the right questions. I'll use a hypothetical example: suppose we brainstormed a big promotional element at SOUL Church and the execution didn't meet my expectation. After I talked it out with a few people, I'd start writing down every question I needed to find an answer to. Stuff like: Who was on point for this? Who dropped the ball? Have they taken responsibility for it? Or are they making excuses? Was I clear about what I wanted? What part did I play in the failure? (Leaders, we always play some part. Probably a bigger one than we think). What broken system caused this? What's our plan to fix it? What's our timeline? These could go on and on and can get much more detailed than this according to the nature of the disappointment. Some questions may have immediate answers. Others may take time to get to the bottom of. And some may have no answer at all for now. Questions are the vehicle to transport your disappointment out of regret into the realm of potential and progress.

STEP THREE: ACTION

Thorough reflection and probing questions can actually do more harm than good if you don't follow them through to the final phase: learning lessons and planning actions. Disappointments are converted from liabilities to assets when we acknowledge them, analyse them, and then pose the million-pound question: What did we learn from this? Become a good steward of your own crazy mistakes. Then follow that question up with this one: What are we going to do about it? Learning a lesson from every disappointment and planning actions to avoid the same disappointment in the future ensures that the price you pay is not in vain. It's just tuition. I love how my friend Bishop T.D. Jakes puts it: 'You win some, you learn some, you only lose some, if you fail to learn.'

I'm told there's only three ways to learn in life. One: your own mistakes, that's costly. Two: other people's mistakes, the cheapest way. But the most costly is number three: we never learn, we keep making the same mistakes.

Sports broadcaster Harry Kalas is famous for once introducing the Philadelphia Phillies outfield player Garry Maddox by announcing: 'Garry has turned his life around. He used to be depressed and grumpy. Now he's grumpy and depressed.' That's not how you want to end up. When things go wrong, when life gets difficult, when the pain becomes too much to bear, how will you keep going? You need to remember what you so often forget.

In Haggai chapter two, the prophet reminded the people of God's faithfulness:

'Be strong, all you people of the land,' says the Lord, *'and work; for I am with you,'* says the Lord of hosts. *'According to the word that I covenanted with you when you came out of Egypt, so My Spirit remains among you; do not fear!'* In these verses, God reminds them that He was with them in the past. He was there when they crossed the Red Sea. He has been their deliverer, and He will be their deliverer again. We are given amazing privileges when we remember what we have in Jesus. Recalling these promises is a good way to maintain our guard against disappointment, even when facing challenges in other areas. Consider the following blessings.

Christ's gift of salvation. No matter what disappointment we're facing, it is microscopic next to the enormity of Jesus' sacrifice on our behalf. The cross was a steep price to pay, but Jesus willingly took our place in order to offer us forgiveness and eternal life. That is worth remembering.

The assurance of God's love for us. The Lord cares for us unconditionally, that is His very nature. Unfortunately, the disappointments of life can cause us to question this, but nothing can separate us from God's love.

Answered prayer. We have the privilege of talking to God as our Father about anything troubling us, and He never grows tired of listening to His children. God is not only able to help us in any situation, He also knows the best possible way to do so.

He has a custom-designed, personalised plan for our lives. The Lord has a will, plan and purpose for our lives that He will accomplish if we obey Him. No one is exempt from disappointment, but we can trust God to bring good from everything He permits to come our way.

Note down some of the promises that we so easily forget in the fog of our disappointment:

- God has promised to supply every need we have
- God has promised that His grace is sufficient for us
- God has promised that His children will not be overtaken with temptation
- God has promised us victory over death
- God has promised that all things work together for good

As we end the chapter, I want to give you some helpful tips to help you take off the mask of disappointment once and for all. There are three steps the Israelites took in Haggai chapter two that serve as a great guide for our own release from disappointment.

Firstly, look away. Don't let disappointment distract you. Haggai 2:3 says: *"Is it not as nothing in your eyes?"* The Jews had to look away from the memories of the first Temple; all they could see was the remnants of the past. Sometimes we have to give up, to go up, and to say hello to something new, we must say goodbye to something old. I wonder what it could be for you. It may be that you need to look away from some painful memory from the past. It may mean that you need to forgive someone. It may be that you need to let go of some dream that is always pulling you in the wrong direction. Not every dream you had for your life was the right dream. As the motivational speaker Zig Ziglar stated: 'Not every door is the right door, some doors are trapped doors, disguised to take you off track and lose your focus.' Regardless of what it is, if it is holding you back, you need to look away. I am convinced that there is no reason for any mature Christian, grounded in the Word of God, to live with a wounded spirit. Looking away says I accept Jesus' death on the cross as satisfactory payment for anything that has happened to me, and instead of me holding the offender accountable, I will leave that accountability in the hands of God. Disappointment breeds like a disease if we don't look away.

The second thing we learn is that we are to look up. Perspective shifts things. "Be strong, all you people of the land,' says the Lord, 'and work; for I am with you." (Haggai 2:4)

Haggai calls the people to look up and turn their eyes away from their pain and away from their problems and their disappointments, but instead to view their situation through the lens of a big God. When your God is big, disappointment looks small. I have discovered that our view of God radically affects how we approach life. Will we understand every disappointment that comes our way? No. But does it offer us a doorway into deeper levels of trust? Yes. Remember that when we wake up, our brain is like a dry sponge, and wherever we apply our brain first, that will saturate us most deeply. At some point in our day, we will be squeezed and whatever saturates most deeply will be what comes out of us.

Finally, look ahead. *"'The glory of this latter temple shall be greater than the former,' says the Lord of hosts. "And in this place I will give peace,' says the Lord of hosts".* (Haggai 2:9). This verse tells us that God only sends your life in one direction: Forward. The Jews in Haggai's day had romanticised the past and completely forgotten the future. What was that future? The future was going to be greater than the former. So many times, we spend our whole lives looking backwards at our mistakes—look forward! As you take off the mask of disappointment, remember your best is still yet to come! There is a reason the windshield is bigger than the rearview mirror. Your future matters more than your past. The empty pages beckon with opportunity and expectation. Fill those pages with stories and adventures, and step into them confidently knowing that God is with you. Right now is the right time to remove the mask of your disappointment! Let's pray.

Heavenly Father, you know what it is to be disappointed. We have all disappointed you at times and fallen short of your standards. Your disciples disappointed you, and even as you wrestled in the garden and asked for the cup to be taken away from you, you willfully surrendered and trusted the heart of your Heavenly Father. Help me to follow your example when I am disappointed, and I will continue to trust your plans and purposes for my life. Amen.

Chapter Ten
– *Sin Unmasked*

I WANTED to finish the book with what I can only describe as potentially the most damaging mask of them all—sin. Whenever we mention the word, we automatically feel dirty, we have flashbacks to maybe something in our past or even our present. For many of us, the word 'sin' can seem confusing, old-fashioned and irrelevant. In fact, if we are to be honest, many of us don't even know what it means. And why would we? It's a term that's not often used in our everyday vocabulary, and when we think about it, we think of church services, with all the hells, bells and smells. In this chapter, we are going to unpack and unmask sin—what it is, how it impacts us and how we can take off this mask that some might not even be aware they are wearing!

An old story tells of a young hunter who lost his life to a leopard that he himself had saved as a pet for his children when the leopard was small and just a young cub. The moral of this tragic story can be easily interpreted from the title: "Little Leopards Become Big Leopards." (Who would have thought?) Sin is easier to deal with before it becomes a habit that eventually takes over and has the potential to ruin our lives. Though this story stands as a picture of profound truth, I believe there is a deeper lesson regarding the nature of sin that is often hidden by the line of thinking adopted by the young hunter. It lies at the essence of the Christian faith and is also the last of the masks for us to take off our faces. The parallel between that small harmless cub growing into a ferocious leopard is similar to little harmless sins being dangerously deceptive and eventually taking our lives.

Whereas the young leopard cub that was brought home to the young family was at first rendered harmless, there is no state or stage or season of life where the development of sin can be said to be harmless. It is always destructive, it is always derailing us, and it is always distracting us from where God wants us to go and from who God wants us to be. Individual acts of sin and wrongdoing are often the symptoms of the true condition of our hearts.

This is why the call to take off our masks and grow in Christian maturity repeatedly zooms in on such small sins and weaknesses like bitterness, rage, anger, harsh words, gossip and malicious behaviour (Ephesians 4:31). Jesus spent a great deal of His time and teaching discussing issues such as anger, lust and frustration, attitudes and mindsets that would not rank highly on our own list of problems in need of urgent fixing. We all have unconscious categories of big versus little sins; we gloss over lists of sins in the Bible because they seem to be of little consequence to our lives as we experience it. Sometimes, if we are to be completely honest, Jesus' teachings can at times seem farfetched and irrelevant to our lives.

The little sins we tend to overlook or not want to address are simply symptoms of a much bigger problem, the source by which we alienate ourselves from God and from others. The masks we wear are a result of these small sins, but they are also the result of our ultimate sin! We are naughty by nature! Me especially! (I feel like I am growing old, just not growing up!) Just spend time with a young child and you will see how naughty we can be! Just chat with someone in prison and you will see how naughty we can be! Just speak to the victims of abuse, betrayal, pain and grief and you will be able to see just how naughty we can be. It's time to take off the mask of sin, as it is stopping us from seeing who we are, who others are, and who God really is! How many jobs have been ruined because of jealousy? How many people have been deprived of genuine help and kindness as a result of the snide comment of someone who secretly disliked them? How many relationships have been destroyed by envy and jealousy? How many countries have been divided because of narcissistic behaviour? How many churches have split up because of selfish motives and ambitions? How much evil has resulted from misinformation or a little colouring around the edges of what they subjectively call "truth?" And have you noticed how much we can control other people just through our body language? The worst enemy preventing us taking off our masks is not the huge everyday sins, but the seemingly harmless sins assumed to be part of what it means to be human. We say things like: 'This is just who I am.' Justifying, condoning and tolerating people's blind spots, instead of speaking the truth in love.

Paul gives us a definition of sin by saying that sin is falling short of the glory of God. (Romans 3:23). Sin is falling short of God's best for us—through our wrongdoing, through our words and deeds. We fall short of the best plans and purposes God has prepared for us. Paul also says that 'everyone' has sinned. Sin is to say: 'God, I don't want you to be my King.' Sin screams: 'I want to be the leader of my own life.' Sin is falling short of God's best by the highest order, and if you turn your back to God, you have fallen short of the King's standards and fallen short of the way are to serve Him. So, have I! But—one of my favourite words in the English language. "But God demonstrates His own love towards us, *"in that while we were yet sinners, Christ chose to die for us."* (Romans 5:8). Christ died to set us who have committed sin (that's you and me) against the King of the Universe, free! What a gift we have been given. What a price that has been paid!

Our human and sinful nature is strong, stubborn and self-centred. It is an attitude that says, 'I don't need a saviour; I can save myself.' It lives the mantra and mindset that "I'll do it my way". When we sin, our focus is all about pleasing, preserving, promoting and gratifying our own longings and desires. Even as a follower of Jesus, I make mistakes—we all do. Under the right amount of pressure, when all the pressures of life are coming down on you, whether it's a deadline that looms or a confrontation with your boss at work, our sin and shortcomings have a tendency to get out. We all try not to let that happen, but we do. What's in us, comes out of us when we are under pressure. Is it nature or nurture? You have a sin nature that you were born with. To echo what one well known evangelist says: "The heart of the human problem is the problem of the human heart."

G.K. Chesterton gave the shortest letter ever to a newspaper editorial. The newspaper invited readers to respond to them by sending in answers to the question: 'What's wrong with the world?' Chesterton decided to write to the newspaper and tell them what's wrong with the world. It was the shortest letter ever sent to an editor, his letter ran: 'Dear sir, I am.' Yours sincerely. G.K. Chesterton. I am what's wrong with the world. It's me. Because we're born in sin, we are the problem. Thankfully, it doesn't end here; there is some good news. Each of us entered the world with a sin nature; God entered the world to destroy sin's power and to take it away.

Sin has five faces and it literally pervades each of our senses. Sin looks good, it tastes good it sounds good, it smells good, and it feels good. Until we see how prone we are to sin, and literally see ourselves as sinners, we will never recognise our need for a Saviour. We could never save ourselves or do this on our own. If we could save ourselves, we wouldn't find any need for a Saviour. Jesus never entered our world to give us tips and 'how to' principles of how we could save ourselves. Instead, He entered the world to save us to Himself. In the boy scout's, you earn a lifesaving merit badge. Realistically though, the only people these young boy scouts get to save in their training are other boy scouts who didn't need to be saved. In the training, you feel invincible. You rescue all the other scouts, and you take turns being saved and being the one who does the saving. But because the boys tend to know they aren't really drowning, they resist being rescued. They kick and scream, and fight and wrestle as they don't want to be saved. It's a beautiful picture of how difficult it is to save those who are trying to save themselves. So often we fight and wrestle God thinking we can do it all ourselves, when in fact the truth of the matter is, we must come to the end of ourselves. We must acknowledge we are not enough; we must take off the mask of self-reliance, and self-dependence, and come out of the shadows and into the light.

Like shame, sin is pervasive, but it's powerful because it's so subtle. According to a NASA researcher, a two-degree miscalculation when launching a space rocket to the moon would send the space rocket 11,120 miles away from the moon (a bit like how living in Norwich is from the rest of the world); all one has to do is take time and distance into account. We cannot build a purpose-filled life on a foundation of sin. He died on a cross for you and for me. He was beaten. Mocked. Spat on. They made a crown of thorns and placed it on His head. They pierced His side with a sword, and the only relief He got from the dehydration He was experiencing from being hung on a cross, was bitter vinegar. He experienced it all for you and for me so we would never have to wear any of the masks we've acknowledged again, but could walk boldly before God, as His much loved son or daughter. Jesus paid for the sin of humanity so we could break the cycle of sin and take the masks off our faces.

Therefore, because Jesus has paid the ultimate price, when we continually walk around in sin, it's like the enemy of our soul wraps us up in grave clothes. I wonder what grave clothes you are wrapping yourself up in today? Clothes of lust. Clothes of comparison. Clothes of jealousy. Clothes of unforgiveness. When we continually walk in our sin, it's as if we go back to the cross of Jesus and take off all the sin and wrong that Jesus put on it! I've noticed in my own life, whenever sin or temptation comes my way, (and it does, being a pastor doesn't make you exempt from sin), the consequences are never worth the momentary satisfaction. When I come head-to-head with sin, I always ask myself this question: Do I want to trade what's in front of me right now for what

I want most? In other words, do I want to trade this bad deal for my financial reputation? Do I want to trade this short term sexual feeling for my wife and children? These questions have helped me numerous times avoid sin because the question is always answered with NO!

Are there any golfers reading this? I'm not a big golfer. I can hit a ball, have some mischief on the golf buggy and enjoy the tidy turf, but I just don't have the concentration levels needed to take it seriously. One of my first memories of playing golf was watching a ball come over the hill onto the green from a different hole. I saw an opportunity to make someone's day, so I ran over and placed the ball in the hole and then hid in the hedge. The golf enthusiast searched long and hard for his ball then eventually looked down the flag into the hole, saw his ball and broke out into a little dance on the green. You can just imagine twenty-five years later he's still telling his grandchildren about his hole in one. You might say what's that got to do with sin? Absolutely nothing. But on a serious note!

Many golfers, probably like my hole-in-one friend, are fans of what is called a mulligan. I don't know what they did or how it started, but they have added something special to golf. Its use is found after you have swung your golf ball. When you slice a shot at a ninety-degree angle to what you expected and the ball lands in a pond, it is at this point Mr. Mulligan comes into his own. Because if you were playing with a friend they would offer you a mulligan. You would get a second chance. You would pretend the ball you just hit didn't exist and you would hit it as though it was your first shot. If our first shot ended up in the pond, and skewed off and is unplayable we get another chance. We have also been given a Mulligan! We have been shown grace after we have fluffed our shot. Wait, it gets even better. Because as humans we don't just need a second chance and a third chance, because we will keep messing up. The human condition is sin, and so we can't just deal with the symptom, but we must address the source. So, God sent His Holy Spirit to teach, train and correct us in our lives. It is just as Tiger Woods would come onto the green, and steady your hand, and instruct you how to take the perfect shot, with his hands grasping your hands and guiding you into making the perfect shot - the mulligan deals with the symptoms, but an instructor deals with the source. God sent Jesus to die on a cross and then sent His Spirit after He rose again so that you and I could be forgiven, set free, and find freedom from our past, our purpose for today and a hope for tomorrow.

How do we make sure our shot at life doesn't end up in the pond or drift into the rough? How do we make sure we follow our instructor's advice and make the best shots and decisions possible? I want to use the acronym **D.R.I.F.T.** to help remind you how to do this.

D – DON'T GET DISTRACTED

We get distracted when we allow the good gifts and blessings God gives us, like success, a business deal, a job or our influence, to become more satisfying than Jesus himself. We drift from Jesus when we're not honest with our negative emotions — like anger, unforgiveness, bitterness, and resentment. We drift when we treat good things as though they are God things. We drift from Jesus when we try to establish an identity based on anything we do, instead of everything Jesus has done.

R–REFUSING TO REPENT

Repent can seem like a big, religious, church word, but it simply means to change your mind and to turn away. To turn our backs on what's wrong for us and move towards the One who wants what is right for us. At the root of every sin is pride and refusing to acknowledge our shortcomings is the quickest way for us to get ourselves in difficulty.

I–INTENTIONAL ACTS OF DISOBEDIENCE

As "The D.R.I.F.T." progresses, we begin to intentionally sin. Instead of sprinting to Jesus to satisfy our needs, we run to other things: work, pornography, people-pleasing, sex, food, self-sufficiency, alcohol and lying. True freedom is freedom from sin, not freedom to sin.

F–FAKE COMMUNITY

The next phase leads to fake community. This is what this entire book has been about, wearing masks to hide who we are and to protect us from being our true selves and transparent with one another. We become numb and fake to others.

T–TREASURING SOMETHING OR SOMEONE MORE THAN JESUS

The ugly offspring of "The D.R.I.F.T." is when we begin to treasure something or someone other than Jesus. The human heart was created to worship. People caught in the clutches of "The D.R.I.F.T." are now worshiping people or things that will ultimately hurt them and those they love.

So, what can we do if we are experiencing "The D.R.I.F.T."? Here are three simple steps:

CONFESSION. Confess to Jesus that you have been drifting and you need Him.

COMMUNITY. Speak to someone you trust within your community and allow God's grace to make you whole.

CHOOSE. Commit to sharing the good news you have received. Help someone who is experiencing "The D.R.I.F.T." Let them know that you have been where they're going and it's not worth it. Give them a copy of this book to help them unmask and move forward.

Let's remember this: Sin has a sweet first bite that becomes more bitter as you go. Obedience has a bitter first bite that becomes sweeter as you go. Sin makes us feel like puppets, pulling us one way and then another, and it controls us. When it pulls us one way, we end up responding and we never feel free of sin. The cross of Jesus is like a huge pair of scissors that comes along and cuts the strings. It cuts them off. Sin tries to pull us this way and that way, but we're dead to the response to sin; the puppet is no longer attached to the string. I love this definition of salvation: No strings attached. I don't want to be the same puppet I was ten years ago, being pulled around by the same cycle of sin and death. We are no longer mastered by sin. I don't want the enemy to think he's mastered me. I am free. We are free from the hold. Nothing can hold on to us anymore if we step into what Jesus has set us free from. When you feel the old tugging away at you, you can say 'no, I am free!'

I don't know how many of you remember English Literature at school; I can because I got a whopping, great big D for my GCSE, and now I am writing a book! Miracles still happen. My English teacher Mr. Den would pass out if he's even still alive! But I remember we had to read a lot of books. One was called 'The Scarlet Letter.' It's about a woman named Hester who is found guilty of committing adultery. As a result, she has to wear a big scarlet 'A' on her dress, as a symbol of her shame. We often do this to ourselves but also do it to others. We can be quick to tag a title or offer a label to someone's actions or behaviours, thinking it defines who they are. When Jesus died on the cross and rose again,

He took our old rags and replaced them with new threads, a new name, a new hope and a new identity. He puts multiple letters on us: **S** – saved. **D** – delivered. **C** – child of God. **R** – redeemed. Jesus knows the worst acts of our lives, and rather than retreat in dismay, He reaches out and offers to give us a fresh start.

Perhaps you are reading this, and you can relate to the scarlet woman—you are wearing the labels of your past regrets, tortured by past mistakes, and as a result you are wearing a mask. Can I remind you that you never have to overcome your broken state to claim God's love? His love has already overcome your broken state and claimed you. You may be guilty, but you will never be condemned. The verdict has been rendered: Not guilty! All you are asked to do is to receive His forgiveness and release control of your life so that you can receive His Spirit into your heart. As you do this, He will transform you into His likeness and He will help you walk in His ways. Christ can be in you if you trust His work for you.

He took your place when He died on the cross. It's now your turn to take off the mask and to give it to Jesus, and He will exchange that mask for a life of purpose and freedom— it is called a crown of glory.

When my children were younger, we had this game called Etch A Sketch—you probably had one to growing up, too. Basically, the kids would attempt to draw all sorts of objects and things (and I mean all sorts :-) and then show mummy and daddy, and like good parents they would always applaud their efforts; but unlike a piece of paper ravaged with drawings and making, the Etch A Sketch could be shaken and instantly all the appropriate and inappropriate removed. I often think that's like our lives; on our own we make a complete hash of it, try to make it on our own, and it just looks like a mess. Then, God comes along and shakes us up, removes all the marks and past the mistakes, and wipes our slate clean.

When anyone was convicted in a Roman court of law, they would be given a certificate of their crimes. It would be nailed to the door of their prison listing every crime, theft, adultery, debauchery. After the prisoner had served their sentence and cleared their debt, the Roman guard would write the words 'It is finished' in red on the certificate, and he would be cleared and never punished for those crimes again. In John's Gospel we read; *'When he had received the drink, Jesus said, "It is finished." With that, he bowed his head and gave up his spirit.'* (John 19:30). When Jesus went to the cross, He took every single one of our certificates with Him. His blood paid for our certificates of sin. When Jesus bowed His head and said 'it is finished', our certificates of sin were paid in full. My past and your past is covered by the blood of Jesus. *'I—yes, I alone—will blot out your sins for my own sake and will never think of them again.'* (Isaiah 43:25). With all this in mind, we must ask the question: If God no longer chooses to remember our sin, then why do we?

The Bible says when you acknowledge Jesus, He acknowledges you. I would like to end this book by offering you the opportunity to take the first step and give your life to Jesus, or to recommit your life back into His hands. As you read this prayer, whether out loud or in your heart, me, my wife Chantel, and our church family have been praying that this book would come into your hands, and that you would use this moment to get right with God, right with yourself, and to take off the masks that have been inhibiting and restricting you from living a life of freedom and wholeness.

Jesus, I am deciding to trust you with my life. I acknowledge that you are the only one who can save me Forgive me of my sins. I repent from my past. I believe you're the son of God, that you died on a cross and you rose again so I could be free. So right now, in this moment as I read the words on these pages, I receive your love. I receive your grace. I receive your forgiveness, and I am asking you, Jesus, to be the Lord of my life. I receive this new life, from this day forward, I am a follower of Christ. In Jesus name. Amen.

Can I be the first to congratulate you on becoming a follower of Jesus? This is the greatest decision you can ever make on this earth. I can't promise you an easy life, but I can promise you God will be with you every step of life's journey, through the good, the bad and the ugly.

Saying the prayer was such an important first step, but can I encourage you to take a couple more?

STEP 1 - TELL SOMEONE
Find someone at school, work, or at the gym who you know is a Christian and let them know you made the decision to follow Jesus. Community is a vital component of the Christian walk. You can't do it on your own!

STEP 2 - FIND A LOCAL CHURCH
Church is where Christians gather together. You can do this either in person or virtually. If you don't know of a local church close by, please reach out to our team at info@soulchurch.com and we will help you.

– Epilogue –

What if you were willing to speak to someone you trust and be completely honest about what's really going on in your world? Imagine a conversation where you can be open and vulnerable about the masks you wear and your desire to remove them. I wonder what a mask-free you would look and feel like? Now that we have diagnosed and removed the ten masks that stop us from living lives of freedom and authenticity, I want to give you four simple statements to live by which can bring freedom and wholeness to your life and give you the strength to live unmasked.

ONE: I AM NOT PERFECT

The apostle Paul writes, *"My grace is sufficient for you, for My strength is made perfect in weakness. Therefore most gladly I will rather boast in my weaknesses, that the power of Christ may rest upon me."* (2 Corinthians 12:9). Paul is writing to the Church and saying, 'Guess what? I don't have it all together'. This is a great example for us as we prepare to live life unmasked. Admitting the truth about ourselves is the starting point of change. Chantel and I are just as imperfect as you. Chantel and I row. We sometimes put others in front of our own relationship and children. We make mistakes. We get tempted. We think bad thoughts. We have wanted to quit leading our church. We have felt threatened by others. I have preached messages I haven't lived out. We eat bad food on Sunday night after church (Gasp! Shock! Horror!). I am learning that being a leader is not always about being strong; it's following Christ in our weakness, and it's He that makes us strong. We don't have to have it all together; let us take off the masks that stop us from being honest with ourselves and others.

We can only take a step towards wholeness when we are vulnerable and honest about who we are.

TWO: I AM NOT LIKE ANYONE ELSE

Paul says to the same church in Corinth: "*Yes, the body has many different parts, not just one part. If the foot says, 'I am not a part of the body because I am not a hand', that does not make it any less a part of the body. And if the ear says, "I am not part of the body because I am not an eye', would that make it any less a part of the body? If the whole body were an eye, how would you hear? Or if your whole body were an ear, how would you smell anything? But our bodies have many parts, and God has put each part just where he wants it."*

This is a clear message: Be comfortable with who you are. There is only one you. When it is tempting to pick up the masks you've taken off, remember what Paul writes to the church: You were created to be you. Often we want to wear a mask to fit in and to become someone else. The most exhausting activity is pretending to be who you aren't. There are no accidents in Christ.

THREE: I AM AN UNFINISHED PRODUCT

"*Being confident of this, that he who began a good work in you will carry it onto completion until the day of Christ Jesus.*" (Philippians 1:6). What Paul says here is really releasing. You're not quite baked all the way through. You'll become who He made you to be, but it isn't an event—it is a process. It is never immediate, but it's incremental growth. Before I got married, I gave the best marriage advice. Before I led a church, I was the best pastor. Before I became a dad I gave the best parenting advice. Humbling ourselves before God admitting we don't quite know what we are doing is really freeing. I don't have it all together. I actually don't know what I am doing, but God is with me, and God is with you.

FOUR: I AM UNCONDITIONALLY LOVED BY GOD

Paul writes in Romans 8 38: *'And I am convinced that nothing can ever separate us from God's love. Neither death nor life, neither angels nor demons, neither our fears for today nor our worries about tomorrow—not even the powers of hell can separate us from God's love.'* Ultimately, why do we wear masks? Because we all have a deep desire to be loved and accepted. In fact, we don't just have the desire; we need to be loved and accepted. We were created by God, to be loved by God and by other people. One of the basic needs of your life is to be loved. I have shown throughout this book that we will at times do anything to make sure we are not unloved. It drives us to wear masks, and I have shown that the antidote to wearing a mask is to trust in God's love. Don't build your self-worth on another person who loves you conditionally. The Bible says, *'Don't be afraid for you are deeply loved by God'.* (Daniel 10:19). Hold on to this truth; memorise it. Let it become a part of you, and let it sink deep into your heart and seep out into every area of your life.

God's love is everlasting, and His love is unfailing. The renowned theologian Karl Barth visited the University of Chicago. As students and scholars crowded around him, one asked, "Dr. Barth, what is the most profound truth you have learned in your studies?" Without hesitation he replied, "Jesus loves me this I know for the Bible tells me so." No matter what failures or challenges life throws at us, one constant is this—He loves me.

Jesus warned us if we cling to our life, we will lose it, but if we give up our life for Him, we will find it. I close this book with the Jon Norman paraphrase of that verse: If I cling to my masks, I will lose my life, but if I give up my masks, I will discover real life. A mask might be a place we can hide, but it's also a place we can die. Let's choose to live with unlimited love and lead an unhindered life.

The outcome of unmasking today is this: the world gets to see the real you. There is only one you with a unique fingerprint and footprint on the earth. As you take off each mask, you will begin to recognise the moments you are tempted to put them back on, but you will be able to resist because of the revelations you have received and what the Holy Spirit reminds you of from this journey. As you keep off the masks, and put on Christ's truth about who you are, your relationships will go deeper and stronger, you will walk with courage and confidence, and the world will get to see the real you—the you that you were made to be, the you that you are meant to be, and the you that God has purposed for you to be! We are on this journey together.

I believe in you.

Jon.

– Dedications –

I would like to dedicate UNMASKED to my dad who graduated to eternity in 2010. I learnt so much from him, a man who loved JESUS with all his heart, and I'm so grateful for his life, his sacrifice and his love for others.

I am beyond grateful for my darling wife Chantel and our two amazing children, Miracle-Joy and Justice-Murray, I love you all dearly. Life with you just keeps getting better and better.

My dear mum Gillian, who has stayed the path, kept the faith and believed in me since day one, I love you.

To my SOUL Church family, whose support and love has been relentless, and to my many friends who have inspired me, challenged me and encouraged me to keep going when I almost quit, thank you.

Finally, I am so grateful for my Lord and Saviour JESUS Christ, without His strength, power and wisdom in my life I wouldn't have made it!

SOUL CHURCH LEADERSHIP ACADEMY

SOUL Leadership Academy is your opportunity to EXPERIENCE serving the local church and to build relationships, to EQUIP you in the Word and a deeper revelation of God, and EMPOWER you to step out in your gifting in a life-giving environment.

Come and join us on the adventure...

www.soulchurch.com/church-life/sla

Experience - Equip - Empower